PRAISE FOR
AS FAST AS HER

"What Kendall Coyne is doing for the sport is not just about her—it's not even just about her team. She is changing people's perspectives about what a woman can accomplish. In *As Fast As Her*, she shares her mission of empowerment, showing all readers how they can open the door to whatever they love and confidently walk through."

Manon Rhéaume, the first woman to play in the
NHL, Olympic medalist, and speaker

"I met Kendall when she was seven years old, when she first had a dream to play hockey in the Olympics. It was a thrill to watch her grow into an elite athlete and achieve her dream of winning gold. On top of that, she shocked the sports world by proving she is as fast as the best men's players in the world. Kendall is an incredible leader, a huge advocate for the game, and the perfect role model for the younger generation. This is a must-read story."

Cammi Granato, member of the Hockey Hall of Fame,
Olympic medalist, and NHL pro scout

"When I first met Kendall Coyne back when she was a young, excited fan, I had no idea what an amazing player and person she'd become. In the years since, I've been amazed by Kendall's focus on becoming the best she can be, her drive to make her mark on the sport and achieve her goals, and her dedication to helping young people grow and see the possibilities in themselves—including her fight to create a better future for women in hockey. Throughout *As Fast As Her*, as she shares the challenges and obstacles she's overcome in her career, Kendall offers a powerful message to any young person who is chasing their dream or working to make their voice heard: Don't let anyone tell you no, and fight for the respect you deserve with everything you have. In the end,

I came away an even bigger fan of Kendall, and hope this book inspires a new generation to follow in her footsteps."

Chris Chelios, three-time Stanley Cup Champion
and member of the Hockey Hall of Fame

"Kendall Coyne is one of the most impactful athletes ever to lace up a pair of skates. While she is best known for her explosive speed, what I admire most about her is her fierce determination, fearlessness, and work ethic. Not every athlete—no matter how gifted—possesses the mental toughness to show up on a big stage. In addition to showing up for Team USA on the international stage numerous times, Kendall's clutch performance at the 2019 NHL All-Star Skills Competition was a shining example of thriving under intense pressure. That lap was a barrier-shattering moment for the women's hockey world, and only someone like Kendall could have pulled it off. Every athlete and sports fan—no matter your age, gender, or favorite sport—will be able to enjoy and learn something from Kendall's story of overcoming obstacles, constantly pushing herself to greater heights, and rising to the occasion when called upon."

Patrick Burke, Senior Director of Player Safety for the NHL

"*As Fast As Her* is sure to inspire, as Kendall is a leader and role model both on and off the ice. As a professional, I have had the honor to work with her to create the 'Golden Coynes' program to welcome youth girls into our great game and help them keep playing. As a mom to my ten-year-old daughter, Amelia, I've seen the impact Kendall has made in helping her to set goals and **dream BIG**!"

Annie Camins, Chicago Blackhawks Senior Director, Youth Hockey

AS FAST AS HER

DREAM BIG, BREAK BARRIERS, ACHIEVE SUCCESS

KENDALL COYNE
WITH ESTELLE LAURE

ZONDERVAN

As Fast As Her
Copyright © 2022 by Kendall Coyne Schofield

Requests for information should be addressed to:
Zondervan, *3900 Sparks Dr. SE, Grand Rapids, Michigan 49546*

Zondervan titles may be purchased in bulk for educational, business, fundraising, or sales promotional use. For information, please email SpecialMarkets@Zondervan.com.

ISBN 978-0-310-77113-5 (hardcover)
ISBN 978-0-310-77685-7 (audio)
ISBN 978-0-310-77114-2 (ebook)

Any internet addresses (websites, blogs, etc.) and telephone numbers in this book are offered as a resource. They are not intended in any way to be or imply an endorsement by Zondervan, nor does Zondervan vouch for the content of these sites and numbers for the life of this book.

Cover design: Sean Grady
Cover photo: Getty Images
Interior design: Denise Froehlich

Printed in the United States of America

22 23 24 25 26 27 28 29 30 /SCC/ 15 14 13 12 11 10 9 8 7 6 5 4 3 2 1

*To my family—your unconditional love, support,
and sacrifice allowed me to chase my dreams.*

---

*To all my teammates, coaches, support staff, and fans—
thank you for pushing me to be my best on and off the ice.*

To the next generation—always follow your dreams.

FOREWORD FROM BILLIE JEAN KING

Kendall Coyne is a winner on the ice and a champion and leader in life. It's not an easy combination to achieve or keep together, but it is an important one. You may have seen her professional level of success, as she was part of the 2018 Olympic gold-medal–winning hockey team and has won an amazing twenty-one medals in international competition. But in this book, she reveals her character—the root of her inner success—that is so important to defining who she really is.

We first met at an espnW event in 2010, but we really got to know one another after she grabbed the attention of the sports world at the 2019 NHL All-Star Game in San Jose, California, when she stepped onto the ice as a last-minute replacement in the skills competition, becoming the first woman to compete in the Fastest Skater Competition. She finished less than a second behind the winner, becoming the fastest woman on the ice. So many times, women only get attention when they do something in a man's arena. It is unfortunate, but it is the reality we face. So you have to make the best of the situation, and Kendall certainly did that. In the quick skate, she showed every boy and girl that if you want something bad enough, you can find a way to make it happen.

That night in San Jose, Kendall's life changed forever. She had done something bigger than hockey, bigger than herself, and it was almost bigger than life; she became a representation of what a woman can do if given the chance. How you handle those moments is part of what defines you.

In October 2019, I joined her at center ice during a Chicago Blackhawks game, where I was supposed to shoot a hockey puck into a very small hole that was set up in front of the goal. It was pretty much an impossible task and more for entertaining the crowd than for demonstrating my skill. I had never held a hockey stick in my hands before that night. I worked for a few minutes with Kendall and her brother Kevin—both of whom showed me how to hold the stick and how to execute the shot.

As Kendall held my arm and escorted me onto the ice, I can tell you my knees were shaking. But she kept me calm. Three pucks were laid in front of me. The first two . . . well, let's just say they were not great attempts. But for the third and final one, I took a deep breath, remembered what Kendall and Kevin had shown me about technique, and I let it rip. It felt like it took a lifetime to reach the net and it was not a thing of beauty, but I think we all almost fainted when the puck slowly disappeared through the hole and into the net. Kendall was jumping up and down and waving her hands. She was so excited, and her reaction showed me how much she loves helping others.

Kendall brings all of herself to everything she does, and she is committed to making a difference in the lives of others. She and her husband, Michael Schofield, founded the Schofield Family

Foundation, which puts community first and helps members of the military, local sports organizations, and families in need. She has gone on the ice to do countless hockey clinics and camps for kids of all ages and backgrounds, and she is leading the charge for women's hockey to have a sustainable professional league and a player's union that will help grow the sport that is so important to her. She wants more girls to have increased access and opportunities in hockey, in sports, and in life. I have long believed that when a woman leads, she does not lead just for girls and women, she leads for all of us—and Kendall is doing just that.

As Fast As Her teaches us how champions win, why dreaming big is important, and how commitment, preparation, and leadership will take you to the next level. It shares Kendall's "never give up" attitude, her commitment to others, and her lifelong belief that we are all stronger together.

BILLIE JEAN KING

CHAPTER 1

NOT THOSE SKATES

*Follow your heart. It will take you
on an amazing journey.*

I was born playing hockey.

I wasn't, of course, but I might as well have been because I honestly don't remember much before discovering the sport. My brother Kevin is three years older than me, and as far as my memory is concerned, I rolled out of the womb and into competition with him. Most likely, we were battling in a game of shinny hockey. What's shinny hockey? It's in the name! The game is just like hockey, but you play it off the ice while on your shins and knees using mini plastic hockey sticks. Prime shinny games happen in homes, rinks, and the hallways of hotels. Since Kevin and I played so much, we ripped holes in the knees of every pair of pants we owned. If we weren't playing shinny, we were rollerblading in our unfinished basement or up and down our street, hockey sticks in our hands. I loved the feel of going fast and the contest of keeping up with Kevin. I loved everything about hockey from the very beginning.

While Kevin was the firstborn child of the Coyne household, his wild nature forced my parents to pick a preschool where there was an escape-proof playground to contain him. He was so energetic that my parents also put him in any sport they could find to keep him busy, and before I was old enough to play on my own team, I was along for the ride.

My entire family grew up in the southwest suburbs of Chicago. My dad, John, worked as a Cook County assistant state's attorney and still does to this day. My mom, Ahlise, worked as a mutual clerk at various Chicago racetracks. Mom watched us during the day while Dad was at the office, and Dad took over at night when Mom went to work. As a mutual clerk, she took the bets and paid out the winners, and sometimes she was gone until two in the morning. She met some wonderful people at the track who loved horses just as much as she did, but on the other hand she had to deal with intoxicated people, people with gambling problems, and people who were upset about losing . . . all sorts of challenging things. She often had so much adrenaline running after work that she would do her grocery shopping on her way home in the wee hours of the morning to give herself a chance to decompress from all the drama.

When Kevin and I were around five and two years old, my parents decided to build a house in Palos Park, Illinois. They knew they wanted to have more kids and needed more space, but they didn't have much money. To save on expenses, Mom was the general contractor. While we waited for our new home to be finished, we rented a house not too far away in Oak Forest. It was more of an empty nester neighborhood, so Dad went looking for some kids Kevin could play with—and in the process he stumbled upon a learn-to-skate program at the Southwest Ice Arena in the neighboring town of Crestwood.

Some of my earliest memories are of standing on my tippy-toes to see over the rink boards while Kevin skated at the Southwest Ice Arena. I studied his every move, jealous he got to be on the ice, frustrated I was too young to join in. Even then I couldn't wait to get home so we could play together. Kevin cut me no slack. He never treated me different from any other kid he competed with. Going easy on me would have affected his entertainment, and I was up for the challenge.

We tumbled and threw balls, and Dad played along.

Dad was already training us in his own way, working on our hand-eye coordination and athleticism by teaching us the fundamentals of baseball, such as running, hitting, throwing, and catching. Intent on giving us proper training, he even taught us to be left-handed batters so we would have an advantage, even though we didn't understand what he was doing at the time.

While baseball was Dad's favorite sport, my parents were all about letting us try anything we wanted to explore. They also never forced us to do anything except have good manners, finish our homework, and—most important to Mom—eat our dinner, so we were free to feel out the world around us for things we might enjoy. When we moved into our new house in Palos Park about the time I was three, we were delighted by everything we could discover. It was the kind of neighborhood that had a ton of kids. We would cross paths with each other on the sidewalks, and later there would be a knock on the door and the same kids would ask to play. When we put our Benny the Bull basketball net in the backyard, all the kids came over for games. We had a decent-sized backyard, but if we got bored there was a farm behind the house where we would roam, or we would wander across the street to the pond and fish using the hot dogs and bologna we pilfered from our refrigerator.

While my parents were excited about finally having a finished product to move in to, if you'd asked me, I would have told you that the best thing about our new home was what *wasn't* finished. Kevin and I would rollerblade in the unfinished basement and shoot pucks against the concrete walls. Upstairs, after bedtime, we would hide in the unfinished fireplace that connected the living room to the family room, so we could see the TV without being seen by the grown-ups. We felt so sneaky and rebellious.

We would also play shinny hockey in the upstairs hallway. Because we had a split level, there were railings over the family room below, and the small, round shinny balls constantly flew over them and landed on our parents. They had a good sense of humor about it, though I'm sure we annoyed them. I have such great memories from living there that my mom always calls it "Kendall's favorite house." I loved it not only because of its quirks but because within those walls Kevin and I really bonded as brother and sister.

Like most hockey players, I lost some of my teeth while playing. Luckily, they were just my baby teeth and they were going to come out anyway. Kevin and I had a Jack and Jill bathroom (meaning it was between our two bedrooms with a door for each of us), and when a remaining tooth was loose, I would march through the bathroom and into Kevin's room, demanding he finish the job and rip the tooth out of my head. Even though I complained about the pain and it sometimes got bloody, he had no problem with this big brother task.

The fun didn't come without a cost. In fact, the cute-looking dimple on the right side of my cheek came courtesy of a slapshot (a hockey shot with a strong windup and lots of force behind it) that Kevin took in the basement. Mom put up sheets between our play area and the storage space, and we were only allowed to play on our side of that boundary, but we often shot balls against the sheets. One afternoon a ball went under the sheet, and while I was on the other side retrieving it, Kevin fired another ball and the blade of his stick caught me right in the cheek. If it hadn't hurt so much, I would have asked him to put one on the other cheek so they could match! The point is, injuries and mischief aside, I was having a blast. Even then I knew that to be fulfilled, I needed to be moving. I needed to be free, playing and competing.

GOLDEN COYNE

Listen to your inner voice. It's always speaking to you, guiding you to your passions.

Shortly after moving into our new home, my dad found out about a brand-new ice rink being built just a few minutes away in the neighboring town of Orland Park. As soon as they opened, they would be offering Learn to Play Hockey and Introduction to Figure Skating classes. In addition, the rink would soon become the home of the Orland Park hockey house league program and the Orland Park Vikings travel program for more experienced players. The new rink would host hockey tournaments and skating competitions in an effort to get both sports up and running in the neighborhood.

In the mid-nineties, not many kids were playing hockey in the area. One reason was that the Chicago Blackhawks were nowhere near as popular as they are now, mainly because the games weren't on TV, which meant hockey wasn't a sport people gravitated toward. But Dad thought hockey would be great because of the experience he'd had with Kevin at Southwest Ice Arena. Kevin was approaching seven and I was three, so Dad signed us both up for classes.

I was in for a shock on my first day. My dad, in keeping with what all the other parents of all the other girls had done, signed me up for figure skating, while Kevin would be continuing with hockey. Rough-and-tumble as I was at home, I didn't mind sitting still to get my hair done by Mom or being put in a cute outfit she liked, but I sure as heck minded figure skating while Kevin was playing hockey.

The Orland Park Ice Arena had three sheets of ice: the NHL rink, the European rink, and the outdoor rink. Figure skating class was held in the European rink. That ice was the softest and about thirteen feet wider than the other two sheets; the hockey classes were held on the NHL rink and the outdoor rink, which was the hardest of all three. (It's a little-known fact that ice can be hard or soft, but trust me, it's a thing.) During my figure skating class, we had to march back and forth in a line. I was only three, but this experience is my most visceral early childhood memory. I remember how much I didn't want to be there. I hated that my skates were different from Kevin's the moment Dad sat us both down on a bench in the lobby and grabbed our feet one by one so he could lace up our skates. Everything in me was saying that I wanted—no, *needed*—to get out of *these* skates.

After my second figure skating lesson, I got off the ice, marched with purpose toward my parents waiting in the lobby, and I said, "I quit." Dad swears I've never spoken those words since. I handed him my skates and turned to Mom and said, "I want to do what Kevin's doing. I need the sport."

I only had a few words in my vocabulary in total and I still managed to say all that, so Mom figured I must have needed to say it badly.

My parents looked at each other and shrugged.

"She needs the sport," Mom said.

Dad thought about the two hundred and forty dollars he had paid for Introduction to Figure Skating class. He thought about how I had only made it a couple of lessons in. He thought about how he hadn't even contemplated putting me in hockey and how silly that seemed now that he was thinking about it.

Mom thought about how Kevin and I roughhoused all over the place. She thought about shinny hockey, roller hockey, and how I always seemed to be in motion; about how I loved to run and compete.

And then they said okay.

And none of us ever looked back.

CHAPTER 2

FALLING IS NOT FAILING

*Fall hard, play hard, work hard . . . and
always get back up ready for more.*

I spent two years falling down, getting back up, falling down, getting back up.

That basically sums up my Learn to Play Hockey classes. Three- and four-year-olds don't have the most amazing coordination to begin with and being on ice in boots with sharp blades attached to the bottoms isn't exactly easy. Along with my new pair of hockey skates, I got a new hockey helmet that had a cage with a place to rest my chin. When I first got the helmet, I couldn't see. When I put it on, my hair was in the way. Back then, I thought my hair looked perfect messy, and whenever Mom tried to pull it out of my eyes, I'd run away as fast as I could so she couldn't touch it. But now, I ran *to* her just as fast, asking if she could help get my hair under control. As a solution, Mom put my hair into a high ponytail to keep it out of my face. Well, after a week in the ponytail, I ditched it like my figure skates. My helmet pressed my ponytail way too hard against the top of my head. Like most moms, mine went into action one day when I came off the ice crying that my head hurt. She took my ponytail out, put in a braid, and my life as the Hockey Girl with the Braid began.

You have to learn how to skate, fall, and get right back up before you can take the next step and join a hockey team with other kids. I don't remember minding a second of it. I was so excited to be doing something I loved—even with the bumps and bruises—that I looked forward to it all.

It's true that some kids quit. But I happened to get really, really lucky, because I didn't learn to skate from just anyone; I learned from Coach Bob Arturo. He made what could have been a scary experience into the most fun anyone could have learning to skate and play hockey. He was creative and hilarious. I looked forward to being in his Learn to Play Hockey classes more than almost

GOLDEN COYNE

It's not how many times you fall, it's how many times you get back up faster, stronger, and more determined.

anything else in my life. He was kind and innovative about finding ways to push kids outside their comfort zones without them even realizing it, and that's exactly why he's been doing it for so many years. In fact, he just retired in 2021! He instilled life lessons that go so far beyond the game of hockey; for example, persevering through the many obstacles placed in front of us, such as the fear that comes with trying something new for the first time, failure, and discomfort. These life skills are an important part of learning because they go way beyond physical skill. And trust me, persevering makes the end so much sweeter.

Coach Bob had a system where he put a colored dot on our

helmets that indicated our level. A blue dot was the first level of the program, and a yellow dot meant we had achieved the highest level, like a black belt in karate, which was where we all wanted to be. Sometimes we would stay at a certain color for a long time before moving on. He never gave participation trophy–type stickers, so we all felt extremely proud when we got a new dot since we knew it had been earned. That encouraged us, because we would be able to play in the house league—organized hockey, on a team with other kids—after we got the yellow dot. This process was protection for us too. He wasn't throwing us on the ice to get demolished before we were ready. He was making sure our skating was on par for our age and level, and then letting us move on when it was appropriate. It was a great program, and I had the best time.

As far as my parents were concerned, lessons were expensive but worth it to the whole family if it meant Kevin and I got to burn off some energy in the afternoons, and we loved it so much we quickly became rink rats. What's a rink rat? Even I didn't know then; I just remember everyone referring to Kevin and me that way! What I did know was the rink was exactly where I wanted to be. (Which is exactly what made me a rink rat—a kid who spends all their free time at the rink.) It was basically my own personal playground with air conditioning, snacks, an arcade, slushies, three sheets of ice, and plenty of space for running. I zipped around everywhere and felt at home.

After one year, I earned my yellow dot and completed the Learn to Play Hockey classes. I was then able to join my first hockey team as part of the Orland Park Ice Arena's (OPIA) house league program. Grandpa Coyne—who we called Papa—gave me my very first hockey bag, which had the number 88 on it for NHL Hall of Famer Eric Lindros. I had seen older players at the rink with their jersey number on their hockey bag. When it came time to pick my very first hockey number, I already knew exactly which one I wanted—88—because it was on the hockey bag Papa gave me.

Dad and Papa were two peas in a pod, and there was nothing that brought them more joy than seeing their kids and grandkids happy. Together, they brought fun new toys into the house. Papa got us a pitching machine upon my dad's request, and Dad got a training parachute. Both were more age-appropriate for Kevin, but I wanted to get in on the action, so Dad would operate the pitching machine for me as well or tie a parachute to both our backs so the resistance helped us develop our speed as we ran. Dad would also run drills that emphasized quickness—the ability to reach max speed in our first few steps. I know all of this may sound a little over the top. Okay, really over the top. But the thing is, even at that really young age, I remember asking for it and loving it because I got to go full blast, as fast as I could.

As my pace as a fast-moving child sped up, so did everything else. There were soon two more kids he'd be able to teach. Around this time my mom was pregnant twice, first with my brother Jake and then with my sister, Bailey. As our family grew from four to six, we became an even more rambunctious bunch, though my parents insist we were all also good-natured, polite, and friendly.

Kevin and I were now busy in organized sports. Baseball and hockey games were on Saturdays and Sundays, and even though Mom is Methodist and Dad is Catholic, we were raised as a devout Irish Catholic family who would go to church on Sunday mornings. There were five churches in the area, and Dad thought it was best for us to alternate between the churches and mass times since we tended to create a little bit of a scene wherever we went. We would all tumble into Our Lady of the Woods one week and St. Michael's the next to give everyone a break from the Coyne crew between visits. After mass, we would climb into the car, and Kevin and I would quickly change into our hockey equipment as we drove straight to the rink for our games. We'd often meet my grandparents there, where they would revel in the joy of watching Kevin and me. I felt so supported and cheered for—I knew my family was always present.

Those years were filled with the pure pleasure of doing something I loved and being part of a busy, fast-moving family. There was no sense that there was anything odd about me playing a sport I adored.

Those were the days.

Simple and easy.

It was school, practice, dinner on the fly or sitting down with the family (always prepared by my mom and shared together), homework, hanging out with Kevin, watching Jake and Bailey grow, and then bedtime. I was also playing baseball and basketball and trying to keep up with whatever Kevin was doing. That was life. Clear and on the rails.

And that peaceful time wasn't *all* because of hockey. I loved school too. I enjoyed getting assignments and doing the work to accomplish them. Flipping to a new page in my assignment notebook at the beginning of the week and knowing what I had to do fit my temperament and satisfied the part of me that liked order. After school, I would immediately do my homework so we could get in the car and zoom to the rink. Since homework was one of the things we had to get done, I always had it done before practice.

I'm grateful I was able to enjoy every second of being on the ice for my Learn to Play Hockey lessons, because they still amount to some of the best moments of my life. I remember the thrill of running into the Orland Park Ice Arena as fast as I could, with my braid flopping in the air and a hockey bag I could hardly carry skimming the ground because of my height. I remember having my mind set on a goal, wanting that little yellow dot so badly, and working hard for it week after week. I had glorious moments making my very first breakthroughs: falling and getting back up on my own, gliding on one foot, striding with two feet, crossing over, and stopping.

Being on the ice is where I belonged. It took effort and required an enormous amount of courage, and unconditional support from the people around me. It was also joyous and filled me with optimism for the future.

Those are the memories I go back to when I need a reminder of why I play hockey, why I belong in this game, and why I've fought so hard since then to demand a space for myself whenever people tell me that being female somehow makes me and others like me unworthy.

I started out falling, have fallen many times since, and I have no doubt I'll continue to fall. But no matter how many times I fall, no matter how many times I get knocked down, I know one thing for sure: I'll always get back up.

CHAPTER 3

HIS MITT AND CUP

*Play as hard as you can, as fast as
you can, and don't let anyone
or anything slow you down.*

It was an afternoon just like any other when the hammer came down on my blissful ignorance of how boys' and girls' sports truly work. We lived across the street from our elementary school, Palos West, and since I was now seven and Kevin was ten, our parents trusted us to walk home together. We usually snacked, watched TV, played Nintendo 64, built forts using the basement couch cushions, and did our homework while we waited to go to whatever sport we were playing at the time. This sunny day in April was the beginning of the new baseball season. Park district baseball was open to anyone, and each year brought a new team and teammates, so I was excited to start.

As you may have already surmised based on the training my siblings and I were getting at home, my dad's sport of choice is baseball. It's important to know that when I say his sport of choice is baseball, I don't mean he really likes it. I mean he is *super* into it. My parents met because he sponsored my mom's sixteen-inch softball team. Yeah. They were called the J's, for John, my dad's first name (cue hand over face emoji). I might not have been quite as into baseball as hockey, but I liked it a lot and I loved practicing with Dad in our backyard. It gave me the chance to bond with him, and I never got tired of fielding ground balls, honing my reflexes, and being outside. I asked him to play catch so much, I think he got sick of me asking. He created this monster!

The start of the new baseball season put a fire in my belly. I still remember the anticipation I felt when the landline rang while I was watching TV in the kitchen. Back in the dark ages, we actually had an answering machine attached to the landline phone, with a speaker that you could hear throughout the house. Because of the answering machine, Kevin and I never answered the phone. Why would we? It was usually someone we didn't know, and if it turned out to be one of our parents, we would leap into action and get to it before they hung up. So as the phone rang, I kept munching my cereal and barely looked away from the television, waiting for the message to start.

Then I heard it: "Hi. I will be Kendall's coach this year in the Pinto Division of the Orland Youth Association Baseball League. We're the Orland Park Expos. Please make sure he brings his mitt and his cup to practice . . .

The coach's voice echoed through the kitchen and I froze. *He. His.* Coach thought I was a boy. Or had he said Kevin? I dropped my spoon and replayed the message. No, he said Kendall, all right. A million thoughts tore through my head. Was it bad that I wasn't a boy? What did it mean that he thought I was one? Did it matter? Was I going to be allowed to play?

In that moment, the call was startling. It's the first time I can ever remember realizing I was different. I thought, *I'm a girl. What does that mean? Why does he automatically think I'm a boy? Is Kendall a boy's name?*

I jumped into the car for my first practice at the John Humphrey Complex in Orland Park on field 7 with my mitt, bat, and baseball cap in place with my hair in a braid coming out the back—because from the first time Mom put my hair in a braid, that hairstyle meant being ready for anything that came my way, be it a baseball practice, a hockey game, or a day at school. I was nervous but I'd been nervous before, like in school when my teacher asked me to read out loud to the whole class. I hadn't let nerves stop me then and I wasn't going to let them stop me now. I also knew Mom had heard the message from the coach because she was adamant about introducing me to him. She got out of the car with me and we both walked up to the field.

The coach looked at me, then back at my mom. He searched past my mom, past me, waiting for a male sibling to appear. "Who's this?" he said, finally.

"This is Kendall," Mom said. "She's here to play ball."

"Kendall? Kendall's a girl?" The coach seemed totally mystified by my presence, and the other parents and players looked on. The field rippled with interest.

He said, "Girls sign up for softball. This is baseball."

"Ok, that's fine, some do," Mom said. "She wants to play baseball and she will be just fine."

Mom then looked down at my stunned face and said, "Go ahead, Kendall. You go play."

I knew right then that I wasn't going to say a word, just like

Mom wasn't going to explain to that coach why I, as a girl, should be allowed to participate in a sport we had signed up for and that I enjoyed. After all, there was no rule that said girls couldn't play baseball. She narrowed her eyes a little dangerously and smiled, and the coach made small talk.

As I ran onto the field, Mom's energy went with me, encouraging me to get out there and do my thing, to let my actions speak way louder than her words. I did just that. I played ball the way I knew I could, just as I had practiced with Dad for hours in our backyard. I could play baseball a lot better than most of those boys. I was faster than all of them too. I had *always* been fast. So I played as hard as I could, as fast as I could, and nobody, including that coach, ever questioned my presence again.

GOLDEN COYNE

Actions really do speak louder than words, especially when you feel like your voice isn't being heard. If you love something, do your best, and don't let anyone make you feel like you don't belong. They may adjust their opinions, and if they don't, they don't deserve your time.

All those people who didn't think I belonged there, including Coach, had nothing more to say after that except, "You're up" and congratulate me as I was chosen to represent the Expos at the All-Star Game.

I often think about why the moment the answering machine went off was such a big deal. It was the first time my eyes were opened to the existence of stereotypes, not just in sports but in so many situations where I would be made to feel like I didn't belong. Hopefully, even in that small case, the fact that I showed up, competed hard, had skills, and helped the team win made him think, *Maybe girls can play baseball,* and then maybe the next girl who came along would feel more accepted and made to feel like she was a valued member of the team. But something was taken from me that day. My certainty about my place in sports that were filled with boys and the equality I took for granted had been changed. I knew something was off about all of it because I deserved the opportunity to be on that baseball team as much as the boys.

That day on the baseball field, I learned that challenging the status quo is uncomfortable but manageable. And looking back, I realized persevering through this had the potential to make this situation better for the next person, and that made it worthwhile even if it caused personal discomfort in the moment. Armed with everything I knew was true about myself—that I was fast, worked hard, and would do whatever it took to do well for my team—I could overcome whatever got in my way.

CHAPTER 4

RINK RATS

It takes a village to be successful.

M y parents worked hard to keep us clothed and fed, as well as be able to support all our extracurricular activities, and most times they were living paycheck to paycheck. Mom stopped working at the racetracks to stay home and take care of the four of us, and instead worked side jobs with flexible hours to help bring in extra money.

Even though she had six knee surgeries, a back surgery, and numerous other procedures from everything she endured during her childhood as a tumbler and a diver, she still got on her hands and knees when she was a cleaning lady and stood for long hours serving lunch to school kids as a lunch lady. She also made flower arrangements while we were growing up. And when it came to the things we needed, both my parents did what they had to do. Mom had a minivan and Dad first had a blue Astro van and then a white station wagon, both of which broke down often but got us from point A to point B. They shopped for off-brand food, bargain clothes . . . whatever had to happen to ensure that they could support the dreams we were eager to pursue.

My siblings and I didn't mind not having fancy things. We didn't get money for hot lunch, receive an allowance for doing chores, or get cash for the school's book fairs. That was okay. The experiences we shared together were always more important to us anyway. We four kids saw the stress our financial needs put on our parents, so we didn't focus like some did on designer clothes, restaurant dinners, or extra training beyond our sports season. And since hockey is one of the most expensive sports my dad could have ever stumbled upon, we were totally on board with having hand-me-down equipment. Dad lived at Play-It-Again Sports, always looking for the best piece of "gently used sporting equipment at a discounted price," and none of us ever gave it a thought. I even found I liked the used equipment because everything was broken in.

I mention all this because I think it's important to understand that Kevin and I, and later Jake and Bailey, were not only super appreciative of what we *did* have, but also focused on what we most wanted: to be at the rink. We wanted to be around the other kids who were rink rats like us, who enjoyed nothing more than being at the rink.

Our rink was the Orland Park Ice Arena, which is now called the Arctic Ice Arena. I still skate and work out there and see a lot of the same people who were there when I was a kid. They love to tell stories about all four Coyne siblings being complete rink rats most of our childhoods. Nobody talks about the kind of equipment we had or how we looked. However, they do talk about the trouble we made for them, especially Jake. No doubt about that.

One time I rallied a group of kids to play sharks and minnows, one of my favorite games on land, ice, or water. In the game, everyone is a minnow except for one person, who starts as the designated shark. The minnows huddle against one wall and try to get to the other wall without being tagged by the shark. That meant running as fast as I could . . . my favorite part! If a minnow is tagged before getting to the other side, they become another shark. The last minnow standing wins.

There was just enough space between the game room and the dining area at the rink to play the game even though there was a No Running sign in plain sight. At that point, I was a minnow trying to get away from a shark, and as was often the case back then, I didn't have my shoe tied. As I was dodging the kid trying to tag me, my shoelace got stepped on and I fell and cracked my head open on the booth in the eating area. Twenty-three stitches later, I had a second battle wound on my face. It complemented my slapshot dimple nicely.

Being in the rink so much, we felt like we were always with people who had similar passions. Jake was mischievous in a completely different and somehow even more terrifying way than Kevin. He would bug the heck out of Frank and Jesus (who both still work at the rink), so much that they would give him credits on the game machines to keep him distracted. All that was fun, but the best part about being a rink rat wasn't the games and slushies, it was the people at the rink who were also like family. Frank and Jesus have worked at the rink for literally my entire existence on this planet. Frank even surprised me with a gift when I strolled into the arena in the wee hours to train on my twenty-ninth birthday. Relationships with my hockey family are some of the most meaningful ones I have. After all, they watched us from the time my parents pushed us into the rink in strollers, all the way until we grew into full adulthood.

And my interest in hockey was blossoming. When I was playing for my first house league team, the Blackhawks still didn't have much of a following and it was possible to get a ticket for seven dollars. Even that was a stretch for my parents with five or six tickets to buy, plus city parking to pay for, so whenever we got to go, I was thrilled.

Although the crowds weren't that big, I loved the noise in the big stadium and watching the players. Chris Chelios was my favorite, so much so that I ditched number 88 after my first year of house league and changed it to number 7 because that was his number. He became my favorite player once I learned he was from Evergreen Park, which was so close to my house. I always thought, *That's going to be me someday.* I knew in my heart that hockey was what I wanted to do, and I felt excited every time I saw someone score a goal and the big horn went off, so excited that I would even stop the shinny game Kevin and I were usually playing to jump up and down and celebrate (because, yes, I would play shinny hockey *even* during a real Blackhawks game).

The Blackhawks had a youth hockey initiative called JuniorHawks, where different hockey teams from around the greater Chicago area were invited to play before a Blackhawks game. You can probably imagine how completely delighted I was when I found out my first house league team, the Jr. Penguins, had been selected to play a JuniorHawks game on the same ice as the Blackhawks. We felt like celebrity players! We got to go into the real locker room, and every player got a jersey with the

Blackhawks logo on the front and their name and number on the back. One team got red Blackhawks jerseys and the other team got white ones.

Since the game started well before the Blackhawks played, the United Center was closed to the public and it was almost all JuniorHawks families and the Blackhawk team employees who were preparing for the NHL game that evening. We even have footage of me playing and Mom commentating. I remember looking up to the Jumbotron and thinking it was the biggest TV I had ever seen in my life. It truly expanded the realm of possibility for me. I didn't know at the time that being on the Blackhawks was something that was almost exclusively available to boys. I only knew that this was something I wanted to do. I wanted the crowd, the cheering, the chance at winning the Stanley Cup not just in my imagination during shinny and street hockey games but in the NHL. I wanted to score and hear the goal horn go off and see the goal light go on, see my image up there on the big screen while hundreds—no, thousands—of people clapped and yelled. While I would play for the JuniorHawks several times over the next couple of years, that first time when I was five was the most memorable.

Playing on the Blackhawks' ice gave me a taste of what it was like to be a professional hockey player. I may have been the only girl playing with a bunch of boys, but it didn't make a lick of difference to me. I loved being surrounded by the twenty-two thousand–plus seats, even if the majority were empty. I lived for the excitement of going through the loading dock and playing in the famous United Center. The feeling I got in this environment brought the whole experience of playing hockey to life.

As the months on the ice soon turned to years, hockey became more and more a part of who I was. It became something I didn't ever want to lose. I only needed my two families: the one I was born into and the one I had found on the ice.

GOLDEN COYNE

It doesn't take an ounce of talent to be a good teammate or friend. Your kindness brightens the world. No smile is wasted.

CHAPTER 5

SEE IT. BE IT.

*Seek out someone who inspires you
and use the inspiration to become
the best version of yourself.*

I had been following Kevin around my whole life and hadn't even realized it. That's just the nature of things when you're a little sister trying to keep up, especially when you have common interests. It was instinctual for me to look up to him and try to follow in his footsteps. I saw him playing hockey and baseball, so I wanted to play those sports too. I tried to be as good as him and as fast as him, and he set the bar high. He was three years older than me, so of course I was always trying to catch up. It gave me a lot to live up to and a constantly moving target, which was excellent for me as an athlete and probably as a person as well.

On February 17, 1998, Team USA and their captain, Cammi Granato, made history by capturing a gold medal at the inaugural women's hockey tournament at the Olympic Games in Nagano, Japan. I was six years old and likely in bed when it happened. I don't remember anything from this game, but I sure do remember everything that happened afterward.

A couple of months later, my parents saw a flyer for Cammi Granato's Gold Medal Hockey Camp for girls of all ages and immediately signed me up. It was the first of its kind. There was nowhere else for girls to experience firsthand what made them icons of the sport. Before Cammi's camp, the only option girls in hockey had to develop their skills was to push through the fibrous layers of a male-dominated environment, even at a young age. And if they wanted to see women play, the only chance was every four years at the Olympic Games.

At first, I was exhilarated I got to go to a hockey camp in the summer. This was a special treat. We didn't do camps or extra training outside the hockey season. We were busy playing other sports and most times camps were too expensive, but this one was reasonably priced because of Cammi's sole purpose of wanting to give back to the game, especially for girls. It was held in Cammi's home state of Illinois—coincidentally mine as well—at the Seven Bridges Ice Arena, which happened to be twenty-five minutes from my house. I was lucky. Girls traveled near and far to attend this unique opportunity.

I had never truly grasped how much my life was centered around my brother and boys and trying to prove myself as one of them, until I found myself in a place that was made just for me. I didn't even know something just for girls in hockey was even possible—until I saw it.

What I did know, however, was that for the first time I was doing my favorite thing with other girls for whom hockey was also their favorite thing, with *women* for whom it was also *their* favorite thing, and all that put together added up to a whole lot of firsts. I could not have been more excited. And best of all, for a whole week Kevin was nowhere to be found. (Sorry, Kevin.) My mindset and goals weren't about following his lead or keeping up with the pace he set. Cammi opened my eyes to a future full of potential, showing me what could be accomplished by girls and women in the sport of hockey.

Cammi was so genuine and authentic. She spent a lot of time with us, making sure we all got the opportunity to be in her presence and really absorb what she was offering, which wasn't only some new hockey skill but rather the chance to see what was possible.

Some people would be protective over an Olympic medal, keeping it safe, but Cammi wasn't like that. She knew it had the power to inspire and teach. One day during the camp, Cammi reached into her hockey bag and pulled out her gold medal so each of us could hold it and wear it. It was that moment I turned to my parents and said, "I want to go to the Olympics and win a gold medal."

As soon as my mom caught sight of Cammi's gold medal and figured out how nice Cammi was, she had an idea. My parents were notorious for unique Christmas cards and would go to great lengths to create themes. On the last day of camp, she ran over to the local T.J. Maxx and found four T-shirts with an American flag on them. She then brought Kevin, Jake, and Bailey along to pick me up from Cammi's camp, put the T-shirts on me and my siblings, and asked Cammi to pose with us. Of course, Cammi said yes. She was patient while Mom struggled to get us to stop squirming, hold still, and look at her for two seconds. We were never able to focus for a full two seconds so we choose the best one, and the picture of us sitting with Cammi became one of the most cherished Christmas cards of our childhood. The one thing that didn't make it into the photo was the medal because it was in Cammi's hockey bag, and even she knew this photo was a one-shot wonder, so if she got up to get it, all four of us would probably be in the four corners of the rink within a split second.

I will be forever grateful for the opportunity to experience a space just for girls at that point in my young hockey career. I don't remember much of the drills or what we did with our days, though I know the curriculum was masterfully designed by Cammi, her teammates, and her brothers. What I remember is how Cammi Granato made me feel. I remember seeing her Team USA hockey bag, tracksuit, and red-white-and-blue hockey gloves. I remember the moments with that medal, when she let me hold it and wear it. I remember receiving my camp jersey with the number 21 on the back and getting Cammi's signature on it. It was clear to my parents that Cammi would be such a great role model and inspiration to me. Dad even laminated a wall-sized autographed poster of Cammi, which I still have today.

Cammi's camp refocused my dream from winning a Stanley Cup with the Chicago Blackhawks to winning a gold medal with Team USA.

GOLDEN COYNE

Maya Angelou's great words are a guidepost for me to this day: "I've learned that people will forget what you said, people will forget what you did, but people will never forget how you made them feel." Be kind and strive to be supportive, generous, and thoughtful.

CHAPTER 6

NOT SO FAST

*Adversity and challenges are the
hurdles of life: run through them,
over them, or around them. Never
lose sight of your goals.*

After Cammi's camp, I returned to the Orland Park House League for a second year in a row, this time with the OPIA Jr. Rangers. I went into the season feeling empowered and confident after meeting my new hero, Cammi, and when the season ended, I was ready for a new challenge. So at seven years old, instead of playing another year in the house league, I decided I wanted to continue to follow in Kevin's footsteps and try out for the AA travel hockey team known as the Orland Park Vikings. Within each age group there were three levels: a gold, silver, and bronze team. It's called travel hockey for a reason—being on any of these teams would require traveling to different cities to play games and practicing more. And having tryouts at all was already a step above the house league, where anyone who signed up got to play on a team, which made the idea of travel hockey feel more intense. Remember, though, we were still pretty young, and while it was getting more competitive the older we got, we were far from being in a cutthroat, top-level situation, so the odds of making at least one team were fairly high.

I went into tryouts knowing I was good enough to make one of the three teams at my age level. With roughly fifteen or more kids on a youth hockey team, that meant there were about fifty kids who could make one of those three teams I was competing to join, in a small town where hockey wasn't that popular.

The odds became even better when maybe fifty kids showed up for tryouts. There was no denying I was the fastest player on the ice, and at that age it meant I skated around everyone else and scored a lot of goals.

After tryouts, each kid got a letter telling them whether or not they made a team. The coaches told us to run away to different places in the rink and open our letters. My mom and dad were there with a camera to capture the moment I got the news. I was sitting with a player named Danny when we tore open the envelopes. He enthusiastically announced that he had made it.

I read my letter, looked up, and said, "I don't think I made a team."

Mom snapped a picture before she had the chance to absorb the information, so there's a picture to immortalize the moment. I processed what I just read as fast as I could. I looked over at Danny, excited for my friend, and then turned back to my letter and felt completely broken inside. I had been cut by every single team. No one had a conversation with me to explain why I didn't make any team.

I was confused and sad.

I picked up my hockey bag in the lobby and started walking to the minivan not knowing what was next. All I wanted to do was play hockey. Right as we started to leave the rink, my dad went to go find the Orland Park Viking's hockey director, Coach Frank. He was being hailed as one of the best new coaches to hit youth hockey in the Chicago area.

Dad is nonconfrontational but he knew what had happened to me wasn't right.

My dad, who is a very logical person, said, "How could she not make *any* team? That shouldn't even be possible from a numbers perspective."

And Coach Frank said, "Coaches sometimes want a right-handed shooter and sometimes they want a left-handed shooter."

Dad's response was, "I get it! But three separate coaches, for three separate teams of seven-year-olds, did not select the only girl trying out for your program because she shoots left-handed? Seriously?"

Coach Frank said, "I don't think she'll ever be travel hockey material."

Even though he didn't want to believe it, Dad knew exactly what that was code for. Coach Frank wasn't talking about my skill level. He was talking about my gender. Other coaches and parents felt my being on a team would cause problems in the locker room, and they didn't want to deal with it. For the tryouts, I went into the same locker room as everyone else and didn't even think about it, because at seven years old we all got dressed in the same place. So far in my short hockey career, no one had ever once told me I would need a separate place to change.

This also began a whole new issue for my parents to figure

out. Up to now, other than the one moment with the Expos' base-ball coach, my gender hadn't been an issue in hockey or any of the other sports I played.

While I thought getting cut from all the teams meant I couldn't play hockey that year, my parents told me I could go back to the house league and play. On some level, I was bummed that some of my fellow rink rats would be moving on without me, but I would take the house league if that meant I could still play hockey. I went back to the house league for my third consecutive season, this time playing for the Jr. Blackhawks, which I was so excited about. Everyone wanted to be on the Jr. Blackhawks and my third time was the charm. Don't get me wrong, I loved my experience with the Jr. Penguins and the Jr. Rangers, but I always wanted to be a Blackhawk.

GOLDEN COYNE

We all face times when people underestimate us or judge us based on their personal opinions or society's perceptions. While that hurts, what is important is valuing who you are and not letting their actions affect what you can accomplish.

A Viking coach from Kevin's age group knew I was cut from every team at my age level. Knowing my skill set, he approached my parents and invited me to be on an independent hockey team called the Thunder, which played out of Bensenville, Illinois. This team was made up of a small group of good players with excellent coaches who concentrated on skating and skill development. Coaches Todd and Cory were extremely instrumental in developing my skating abilities and skills. Everything happens for a reason.

———

In Illinois, there are three tiers of youth hockey: house league, AA, and AAA. I was already in my third year of house league, and the game was getting too easy; I was the best player and wasn't being challenged enough. I scored two or three goals every game, and I could skate around players with ease. The following season, it was clear the house league wasn't a fit for me, but my parents knew the AA Orland Park Vikings were not an option. AAA is the highest level and the most competitive. It is so competitive that there were only four AAA clubs in all of Illinois. In 2001, I was still too young for AAA based on the youngest age level available, but Kevin continued to progress in hockey and decided he would leave the Vikings to try to make the jump to AAA hockey.

That's when my parents asked if I wanted to try out for the Chicago Chill AAA Hockey Club, the same organization Kevin was trying out for. One of the main reasons my parents even asked was because they knew that Coach Larry, who was slated to coach the team I could potentially make, was an excellent coach. The other reason was for the possible convenience of Kevin and me playing at the same place. Once they planted the AAA seed in me, I couldn't stop asking when tryouts were. The worst that could happen was getting cut like I'd been before, and I was willing to take that chance.

In hockey, kids are organized by birth year. It's so much a part of hockey culture that when we would go to the doctor's office or register for school and someone asked my mom how old we were, she would rattle off, "Eighty-nine, ninety-two, ninety-five, ninety-six . . ." People would give her blank stares, thinking she was telling them Kevin was eighty-nine years old, I was ninety-two years old, and so on.

When Kevin and I decided to try out for the Chicago Chill, ninety-ones were the youngest team. Since I was born in 1992, I tried out with the ninety-ones. As the only girl at tryouts, I stepped onto the ice and played the way I knew I could.

My parents heard rumblings in the parking lot as other families discussed my presence.

Did you know there's a girl at tryouts?
Yes! I can't believe it!
Girls can't play at this level!

Thank goodness my parents let me attend the tryout regardless of the negativity they were hearing. They supported me unconditionally in the things I wanted to do. What would have happened to me if I hadn't had the parents I did, parents who supported me no matter what, even if it meant looking different to others?

The tryout was hard. There were a lot of good players on the ice, and I didn't know a soul. I didn't expect to know anyone, though, because it is extremely rare to go from house league directly to AAA, and the Chicago Chill's home rink was over an hour from my house. The tryout itself took place over three nights. The drills were difficult. The pace was much faster. All the players were very skilled. There was much more passing, shooting, and skating than I was used to. Sometimes the drills even incorporated more than one puck, transitioning from offense to defense. While everything was a much greater challenge than what I was used to, none of it intimidated me. I understood the drills and pushed the pace using my undeniable speed, and while I'd never had to think about the game at that pace before, I wasn't a second behind. In fact, I was a second ahead, anticipating the plays before they happened. We scrimmaged at the end of each session, and that's really when my skills shone.

The players treated me like anyone else. I got dressed in the same locker room as them and no one gave me any trouble. It was hushed in the locker room all three days; everyone was nervous and awkward.

With the combination of my speed, skill, and hockey IQ, I had high hopes after the third and final tryout day, when Coach Larry met with each player to tell them whether or not they had made the team.

I did.

This already felt bigger, better, and more important than my previous experience.

The following week we had our first team practice as the Chicago Chill '91 AAA Team. We also had our first team meeting, where we tried on what would be our new team tracksuits and team jerseys. We got to pick our numbers, and I quickly secured number 7 for Chris Chelios, even though he was wearing number 24 on the archrival Detroit Red Wings by this time. He was still my favorite Blackhawk.

Yes, I was the only girl on my new team, but never once did anyone on the Chill make me feel that way. At times, we would walk into the rinks together, me with my hair in a braid and a hockey bag dragging on the ground, and parents and players from the opposing team would say:

> *Hey, there's the girl.*
> *She doesn't belong here.*
> *Hit her as hard as you can.*
> *Pull her hair!*

If any of my teammates, teammates' parents, or coaches heard this on or off the ice, they had my back. Coach Larry never treated me differently than the boys either, except maybe in one respect. I like my skates tied supertight, and at nine years old I needed help, so Coach Larry helped me.

My first experience in AAA hockey not only challenged me, it made me feel accepted as a hockey player. Sometimes I wonder what might have happened if I had made that AA travel team with the coach who didn't care about my development. Would my teammates not respect me because he didn't? Would that have sent a message to all the boys that girls in hockey didn't deserve respect? Would I love the game as much as I do today? I'll never know exactly, but what I do know is competing at the AAA level with teammates who viewed me as an equal and a coach who treated me as a valued member and cared to develop me just like any other player on the team made me love the game more than I thought was possible. It fueled my competitiveness and drive to work hard.

CHAPTER 7

ROAD TRIPS

*You won't remember all the wins and
losses in your career. What you will
remember are the experiences
you had during the journey.*

During Kevin's and my first year playing with the Chicago Chill, I was in fourth grade, and we had moved out of Kendall's Favorite House because it was too expensive. We were back in a rental home, just like when I was a baby, except this time I remember all of it. Our tiny rental home was in Oak Forest, the same neighborhood we'd lived in when my dad first signed Kevin up for the learn-to-skate program at the Southwest Ice Arena. This rental mainly consisted of a small kitchen and family room, a hallway too narrow to play shinny hockey, and three tiny bedrooms: one for my parents, one for the boys, and one for Bailey and me. We didn't have a dishwasher, so doing the dishes for a family of six was the worst chore and the one we all tried to avoid being assigned. We didn't even have dressers, just plastic bins from Walmart. When Kevin and I made this massive commitment to play AAA hockey, Mom made a massive commitment too: building another (much smaller) home.

Our schedule was hectic for sure, but we got used to it. We would head to the construction site so the bus could pick us up for school. After a full day of school, the bus would drop us back off at the construction site. Sometimes we would see progress from the day's work, but we almost always saw Mom in overalls and construction boots. After work, Dad would come to the construction site to pick up Jake and Bailey so Kevin, Mom, and I could then make the hour-long commute to Vernon Hills. Mom would drop both of us off at the rink, where Kevin would head off to his practice and I would eat dinner and do my homework in the Vernon Hills Ice Arena lobby. When Kevin was done with practice, we would flip-flop—he would eat dinner and do his homework in the lobby and I would head to practice. During this time, Mom ran to Home Depot or did whatever errands needed to get done for the house. After a busy night for all of us, Mom would pick up Kevin and me at the rink and we would drive home. I used book lights so I could keep working as we drove in the dark. It was rigorous and intense, but it meant I could play the most competitive level of hockey, so I don't remember minding any of it.

Since Kevin and I were both playing for the Chicago Chill, Mom somehow found the time to be the manager of both our teams. That meant she scheduled Kevin and me to play in the same tournaments, in the same locations, and on the same weekends, which I loved because my '91 team traveled with and got to know Kevin's '89 team.

We went near and far: Detroit, Toronto, Pittsburgh, Wisconsin, and Minnesota. We drove the ten-hour trip to Toronto multiple times in the minivan, where we had assigned seats and a VHS player. I loved it because I had my own little storage container where I kept my Gameboy, homework, pencils, and sometimes a CD player, and I was nice and secluded in the back corner. Usually, we watched Kevin's favorite movies, which became mine by default: *Mystery, Alaska*; *Slap Shot*; and every Adam Sandler movie out at the time. While we were definitely too young to be watching those movies and *definitely* too young to get any of the jokes, they kept Kevin busy, so we watched the same ones over and *over*. Many of the lines are engrained in my head to this day.

Since cell phones weren't a thing and we were young kids running wild in hotels, playing shinny hockey and messing around between games, Mom would give Kevin or me a walkie-talkie so she could always communicate with us or know if we were out of range. One time Kevin's walkie-talkie channel turned out to be the same as the one used by a nightclub close to our hotel in Detroit, and Kevin started using the walkie-talkie to allow people in. We thought we were so rebellious and extremely clever.

And at the same Detroit tournament, Kevin was playing against Chris Chelios's son, and I caught a glimpse of Chris Chelios hiding in the Zamboni room watching the game. I was so excited I'd spotted him that I ran to the pro shop and found a Chelios Detroit Red Wings action shot he could sign. The problem was, my parents would *never* buy stuff like that. Ever. So I began convincing Dad I had seen Chris Chelios and this was my one and only chance in life to get his autograph, even though I don't think Dad believed me for a second because he already knew that I had his autograph and had been stalking Chris Chelios since I was five. Dad eventually gave in. I grabbed my new unsigned photograph, then ran as fast as

I could to where Chris Chelios was standing. When he signed my photograph, I was so excited, only to walk away and look down to see he signed with the number 24 he was currently wearing with the Red Wings—not the number 7 he'd worn with the Chicago Blackhawks and the number 7 I wore for him. I ran back to Dad as fast as I could, crying. I explained to him what happened. He said, "You'll be okay." That photo has been on my desk ever since.

Once when we traveled to Toronto, we stopped at the Hockey Hall of Fame. It was amazing seeing hockey's rich history up close. Ever since going to my first Chicago Blackhawks game, I was hooked and would watch as much hockey as possible and learn what I could about the players and the history of the game, so I was excited to be in the place where all of that history came together. At the time there weren't many women featured in the Hall of Fame, but I didn't really notice that. I got a Velcro red-and-blue trifold flip wallet with the Hall of Fame logo and hockey players on it. I didn't want to ruin it and I never had any money to put in it, so I never used it. It's still in mint condition to this day.

Since the US dollar exchange rate made things cheaper in Canada at the time, my parents would use any trips to Toronto as an opportunity to go to the local hockey shop and stock up on as much as they could afford for the four of us, since Jake and Bailey had now started playing hockey as well—anything on sale, like skates, helmets, or gloves. They even bought two hockey nets for the new house being built. Let me tell you, a ten-plus-hour drive home from Toronto to Chicago with two hockey net boxes practically piercing my shoulder was no fun, but to have two hockey nets to shoot pucks into forever was so worth it. We still have those hockey nets in my parents' unfinished basement. Unlike my wallet from the Hockey Hall of Fame, those are *not* in mint condition.

The amount of travel we were doing had increased our family's expenses and created more intensity in our lives, but it wasn't just that. Everything else had ramped up too. Coach Larry was taking hockey to a whole new level for me. He implemented sessions called "skate-ups." Every other week I skated with players who were two years older than me. This forced me to be a great skater—I had to either keep up or get off the ice. I kept up. Coach Larry also defined what it meant to win and lose as a team. As long as we worked hard, the mistakes were fixable; but if we didn't give our best effort, well, we would hear it and he would go extra hard on us at practice the next week. Coach Larry didn't settle for anything but the best from anyone, including himself. The drills he had us do in practice had to be done at full speed. While he was explaining a new drill, I had to give the whiteboard my undivided attention and keep my eyes on the dry erase marker as it went in a thousand different directions, as otherwise I would get lost and have no idea how to do it. If you didn't know the drill, your last hope was to hang at the back of the line and watch the players ahead of you.

He gave the team a playbook, and we had team chalk-talks to go along with it. Even though we didn't use chalkboards, we called them chalk-talks because most of the meeting was spent breaking down the game of hockey on the dry erase board and asking questions. Coach was all about systems, face-offs, reading the opponent's strengths and weaknesses, and understanding the finer details of the game. I loved it.

Coach Larry explained hockey in a way that was strategic and allowed me to think about it from a more advanced viewpoint, but he also gave me far more information than I had access to before. If you didn't understand something, he would encourage you to ask so he could explain it another way. I am naturally a detail-oriented person, so this was like giving me the key to the kingdom. Now I could really dig in and understand the game I was playing. In other words, I went from a regular math class to an AP calculus class while in fourth grade!

GOLDEN COYNE

Never give anything less than your best.

While Coach Larry was teaching us the finer points of the game, he was also teaching us the discipline it took to be prepared. It wasn't just about showing up to practice and performing on the weekends. What we did when we were away from the rink mattered too. For example, when we were staying in hotels, the number one rule was no swimming because it would tire our legs out before the game. I was saving my legs for the ice, but there was another reason I was happy to give up swimming at the hotel. From the time I was nine and started traveling for hockey, I never once took a bathing suit and never thought twice about it.If we had been allowed to swim, my bathing suit would have been different from my teammates and I wouldn't have liked that. Besides, for hockey kids, the best things about hotels are the long carpets and halls to play shinny.

My first experience with AAA hockey opened my eyes to the commitment necessary for playing at the highest level. While I was only nine years old then, getting a taste of being with the best and competing against the best planted a hunger in me. I learned that there were many aspects to the game, and that it wasn't all about what happened on the ice. I learned how to balance school and hockey. I had to be able to focus inside the car while doing my homework to make sure I kept my grades up, because otherwise my parents wouldn't let me continue to play. I also learned to be conscious and appreciative of the effort made by those who were supporting me as I got older and became even more dedicated to hockey. Those experiences were only the beginning of a long road toward becoming the person and athlete I am today.

CHAPTER 8

NO PLACE LIKE HOME

*Be your authentic self. No one else is
you, so be the best you possible.*

The following year, we finally moved out of the rental home
and into our new house that Mom had worked so hard to
build. Bailey and I shared a room in our new home. We had a
bunk bed; I slept on the twin-sized top bunk and she slept on the
queen-sized bottom bunk. I don't remember how that deal shook
out since she was six when we moved into the house, but it stuck.
Honestly, I probably thought it was so fun to jump as high as I
could to get into the top bunk. I don't recall using the ladder once.
And if I was ever too tired to bounce on the edge of her bottom
bunk and jump onto the top bunk, I would nap on her bed.

Just like our old house, we had an unfinished part of the basement and that was the best part of the house to us—because it
was the puck-shooting room, complete with the hockey nets we
purchased in Canada.

That same year, we received exciting news when the Chicago
Chill announced they were moving out of the rink in Vernon Hills

and to the Arctic Ice Arena in Orland Park. Yes, you read that correctly. *To my home rink that was now only ten minutes away!* It was a blessing for my parents. Now Kevin and I just had to make the team. Being a year later, a '92 team was now an option, so I tried out for that team with players my age, and Coach Larry was again the coach. I made my team and Kevin made his. This new team treated me just like the last.

After my second year with the Chicago Chill, it was time for middle school. I was nervous and excited for sixth grade because starting middle school meant a new building with a ton of new kids and teachers. There were two elementary schools in town: Palos East Elementary and Palos West Elementary. Kids from both schools came together at Palos South Middle School, which meant the student body would be much bigger and I would know fewer people at first. But the upside was that our new home was literally next door to Palos South, which meant I got to walk to school every day and we had our own personal baseball field whenever the school wasn't using it.

I had loved my time and my teachers at Palos West Elementary. I was used to getting good grades and was nervous about being able to maintain them, since middle school was much more challenging. Just like in hockey, I hated to fail.

In middle school, I wasn't especially social, although I wasn't a total loner either. At first, I had been excited to find a group of boys who all played hockey together, but they weren't welcoming because I was a girl and I didn't play on their team. In fact, they were all playing AA hockey, which meant I was actually playing at a higher level than them.

Rather than explain, I decided not to trifle with them. I wound up making a few friends who weren't hockey players but were as driven as me. Anila was a tennis player, Taylor was a gymnast, and Elise wasn't an athlete but was passionate about school and became a fierce and supportive friend. Both of the athletes were, in their own ways, on missions like I was. I was so serious about hockey, I gave up chips and pop (what you call soda in parts of the Midwest), and started consciously making healthier decisions. I saw Kevin make decisions like this, so I did too. I was looking for any slight edge I could get, and that meant hydrating well, making sure I got the rest I needed, and asking Mom to pack fruit and water in my lunches. I was ready to do whatever it took to be the strongest, fastest version of myself.

I started to realize not everyone was going to understand the passion I had for hockey or get my Olympic dream, and that was okay. Maybe not every parent was going to love that I was playing hockey, but mine did. Maybe not every hockey player was going to have my back, but my teammates did and so I would have theirs in return. Not everyone at school understood me but I had friends whose dreams I could help support and who would support mine in turn. I was beginning to understand how healthy relationships could help me achieve my dreams. I was beginning to understand that I could only be me. That being true, I set out to be the best, most authentic me I could be.

Perhaps that's why when my parents saw an advertisement that the United States women's Olympic team was playing the Canadian women's Olympic team locally in preparation for the 2002 Olympics, Mom called Coach Larry and said I wouldn't be at practice. When I saw Team USA come out of the tunnel and step onto the ice, I turned to Mom, jumping with joy. "That's them!" I was filled with admiration and the dream I could be one of them someday.

My parents knew watching this game would be pivotal for me, and it was. It was the first time I'd ever seen a women's hockey game and they were playing at the United Center, where the Blackhawks played! Up until that point, the only live hockey games I'd seen were between the Blackhawks and their opponents. At NHL games I'd followed Chris Chelios's every shift, but at this game I was following my hockey camp coach, number 21, Cammi Granato. And for the first time ever, I didn't even bring my shinny sticks to the game. I was like a bug on the glass as I watched every minute, knowing I wanted to play for Team USA one day.

GOLDEN COYNE

Make sure your friends are supporting you, not tearing you down. It's better to have one or two friends who matter and truly care about you than a whole bunch who don't.

CHAPTER 9

THE SOFTBALL ESCAPE

Don't be one-dimensional. Be open-minded about trying new things.

While I loved hockey with my whole heart, summers were for the ball diamond. There were some kids who trained for hockey year-round. Their parents would spend a ton of money for strength coaches to work with them off the ice and skills coaches who would train them on the ice. Those options weren't realistically available to me for financial reasons, but even if they had been, I wouldn't have done it. I was so focused on hockey from August through April that come summer I needed to take a break. I always played baseball for the town, but once I was ten, I was ready to play on an all-girls team, so I changed to travel softball.

Softball was my escape. Everyone knew I was the hockey kid and supported me, though my coach always hoped I would change my mind. While I was playing hockey in the fall, winter, and part of the spring, my softball team would practice their skills indoors. As much as I wanted to be in two places at once, I couldn't balance both with my hockey schedule, so the team was understanding of the fact that I would miss indoor training and join the team in April. It was my summer sport. Softball is all about the heat and sun and going from game to game all weekend long. While softball may have been my break from hockey, there was nothing relaxing about summer softball season. It was go-go-go as usual.

GOLDEN COYNE

If you love sports, try as many as you can. Always be open to new things. When a door to a new opportunity opens, run through it as fast as you can!

The rigors of AAA hockey made me so excited for my first year of girls' travel softball! Ironically, the team I played on was called the Oak Lawn Ice. I guess I couldn't get a complete break from ice! Oak Lawn was where my parents grew up and my Grandma Coyne still lived. I was one of the only players on the team who wasn't from there. It was a very blue-collar town filled with hardworking people, and that was the build of our Oak Lawn Ice team as well.

In hockey, while the boys on my Chicago Chill team accepted me, oftentimes our opponents on the ice didn't. They would try to pull my hair, called me names (*tomboy* seemed to be their favorite), and try and hit me into the boards extra hard. When I played softball, I didn't have to worry about those things when I got to the field. My teammates and opponents accepted and respected one another.

And when we played in tournaments, it was a very different experience as well. One of my favorite parts was when my parents were able to come, because that meant Bailey could be the team bat girl. She had a matching uniform and everything. Bailey would even march out to home plate for the coin flip! She was our lucky charm.

I was the catcher, so I was involved in every pitch and every play, and I was the leadoff hitter as well, which meant when we got to bat for the first time in the game, I was first. Being a left-handed batter in softball was a huge advantage since the left-handed batter's box is closer to first base, so I'm thankful Dad switched me to being a lefty without me even knowing it. I was famous for laying a soft bunt down the third-base line, far from both the third baseman and the pitcher. Even if the third baseman played tight on me, more often than not I had the speed to beat her attempt to throw me out at first base.

I even remember that at one tournament an opposing team made up a code—"shift seven"—to try to get me out. Seven was my softball number, just like my hockey number. The coach would scream, "Shift seven!" when I came up to bat and the players would creep in very close to the batter's box to try to anticipate the bunt and get me out. And it worked—once, they threw me out at first after a bunt that game. I still give them props for the solid defense.

When we played an opponent for the first time, they didn't know what type of speed was coming when I walked up to the plate. Sometimes the coaches couldn't believe how fast I was and would complain that I was out. Our first base coach would chuckle and say no, she really is that fast. After the game, other coaches would make comments about my speed and tell my coach I had a bright future in softball, and he would chuckle again and say, "I'm afraid she's a hockey player."

Given that travel softball was as hefty a commitment as travel hockey, I would often get dropped off at the start of the weekend with our family friends the Gables. Lauren was my teammate and her dad was one of our coaches, but my family and I first got to know them because both Lauren and her brother Timmy played (you guessed it) hockey. If the Gables hadn't taken care of me on many weekends while my parents were shuffling between Kevin's, Jake's, and Bailey's schedules, I wouldn't have been able to play travel softball. Lauren was as small as me and even tougher. Mr. Gable was a big fisherman. Before every tournament, he would pack up our turkey-and-cheese sandwiches and fishing poles, while Lauren and I would burn music onto a CD that Mr. Gable did not want to listen to, and we'd load up the minivan and head out for a long weekend of competition in the sun.

When we got to the tournaments, he would seek out whatever water he could find so we could spend the few hours we had between games eating our sandwiches and fishing. If we couldn't find a place to fish, we'd head back to the car to grab our blankets to sit on, open our coolers with sandwiches and fruit and drinks inside, and hang out as a team. Sometimes we would play cards and make up other games to pass the time until our next game. Remember, this was before cell phones and the iPad! It was hot and humid like a Midwest summer gets, and we would be sweaty and filthy, and it felt great. There was something so carefree and fun about it all. Those are some of my favorite childhood memories.

After the softball tournament I would get dropped off at Grandma Coyne's house and hang out there while I waited for my parents to come from wherever they were with Kevin, Jake, or Bailey. I got to spend a lot of time with my grandma that way.

I enjoyed talking to her about her time as a professional roller derby player. Grandma liked to be fast—just like me. That meant something to me, and those moments were different from the regular school year.

I played with the Oak Lawn Ice for three years. I loved not having to explain why I was there, why a girl was playing a "boy's" sport, or why I loved it. I could just be myself for a few months out of the year. It meant a lot to me: they became like yet another family, and Lauren and I are still friends to this day.

But when August rolled around, the weather started to change and school started back up, which meant my cleats became skates, my sun became ice—hockey was back!

CHAPTER 10

MEETING MANON

*Being the first of something can be scary
but making sure you're not the last by
paving the way for the next is the most
important thing you can do as a first.*

A s my sixth-grade year began, and I started my third consecutive season with the Chicago Chill AAA team, Manon Rhéaume, an Olympian and the first woman to play in the NHL (for the Tampa Bay Lightning), contacted my parents. As the head coach, she was inviting me to be a part of the historic Team Powerade, which would be the first all-girls team to play in the Quebec International Pee-Wee Hockey Tournament. That tournament is comparable to the Little League World Series and is famous for being a sensational event filled with big talent. Players like Denis Savard, Wayne Gretzky, and Sidney Crosby made their first big debuts there, and twenty years earlier Manon herself had been the first girl to ever compete in the tournament, after they changed the rules that year so she was allowed to play.

How in the world was Manon Rhéaume contacting me? I

don't know exactly how she found me, but looking back, it makes sense since I was one of the few girls playing AAA boys' hockey, holding my own at such a high level, and that was enough to draw some attention. I didn't think through any of that, though, when the call came. I was nothing but excited. I couldn't wait. This would be the first time I had a woman as a head coach or even saw a woman coaching, and the first time that I played on an all-girls team. I had to miss two weeks of school and went on a plane for the very first time. Mom went with me. I remember my ears hurt so badly, I thought they were bleeding. I swore I'd never get back on a plane ever again.

GOLDEN COYNE

If you get the opportunity to do something exciting and new but scary, jump on it. Taking those leaps of faith will lead you to success and open new doors. These opportunities can lead to some of the most fun you've ever had.

When we got to Quebec City, we discovered my equipment didn't make it with me—and my new teammates and I had an exhibition game almost immediately at one of the most amazing rinks ever, right in the center of a mall with a huge rollercoaster. It was so cool, but I was devastated at the reality I would have to watch the exhibition game since I didn't have my gear!

We were supposed to play against a local boys' team looking for a practice game, which was important since none of us had played together before, so that made not being able to play even more difficult. Twenty countries were participating in the tournament, which meant there were a lot of teams, and everyone got there early, so what better way to spend our time than playing an exhibition game?

Our assistant coach, Jeff Turcotte, was also coaching the California Wave AAA boys' team, which was playing in the tournament as well. After coaching his boys' exhibition game, he walked down the hall to our locker room and found out I didn't have my gear. He went right back to the boys and told the smallest player to hurry up and take off his equipment. The player didn't hesitate to oblige, and Coach Jeff ran it down to me. As he threw me the bag of sopping wet, smelly gear, he said, "Get ready, kid." I was so excited I was getting to play that I didn't even care everything had just been used. To my surprise, the gear Coach Jeff brought me actually fit. I found out it belonged to an eleven-year-old phenom from California named Rocco Grimaldi, who's currently a forward on the Nashville Predators. I've always followed his career, and as he's an undersized player like myself with a work ethic and heart like none other, I always root for Rocco. He didn't need to share his stuff. In fact, to this day he might not know who he shared it with, but I'll always be grateful. Neither of us needed to *be* big to *dream* big. Rocco followed his dream, and it has led him to an outstanding career in the NHL.

While we were in Quebec, Mom stayed at a hotel while I lived with a billet family who hosted players at the tournament year after year, so it was a tradition for them. One of my teammates was with me, which was great because it made me feel more comfortable and I got the chance to know her better than I would have otherwise. Since Quebec is a French-speaking Canadian province, the language barrier proved somewhat challenging, but

I enjoyed hanging out with my billet family, who lived on a military base and were wonderful people for opening their home to two young hockey players.

In some ways, it felt like I was living in a dream. ESPN followed our team around and made a documentary about us, in which I said, "I want to go to the Olympics!" At night I would write in my journal. I did my best to keep track of everything that was happening, including my dreams and aspirations.

My teammates and I were having a great time during the tournament and I felt welcomed, but then the tide turned. Spectators started throwing hot pennies onto the ice near our bench during our games. I didn't know why at first, but I eventually found out it was because the pennies would quickly melt into the ice and if our blades went over them, we would trip and fall. Skate blades should never step on anything but rubber and ice, and definitely not metal or pennies. Not only does metal dull the skates and ruin blades, we could have seriously hurt ourselves.

People also shouted at us. I didn't know what they were saying because it was in French, but my mom, who had befriended someone who spoke the language, was told that they were screaming girls should be in the kitchen washing pots and pans and we didn't belong there.

We didn't quite realize the magnitude of the issue for the locals at the time, but we were in the iconic Colisée Pepsi and the spectators were incensed by our presence there because we were the first all-girls team to ever play in the tournament. If they'd given us a chance, they would have realized they were watching some very talented, history-making players. So many of my teammates continued to be trailblazers and so many of them went on to have amazing careers; I am incredibly proud to have been there with them at that time.

In spite of the negativity, our time together was so special. I became especially close to three girls: Liz, Alyssa, and Jordan. We immediately clicked and just had a blast together. We were also the three "underagers," so we stuck together because we were excited we would be coming back next year. Jordan was a solid defenseman from Colorado who didn't take crap from anyone. Alyssa was another great defenseman from Raleigh, North Carolina. I'd never known anyone from North Carolina, and because it was so different from anything I'd ever known, it automatically made her cool. She was a big Carolina Hurricanes fan but otherwise she was so sweet, kind, and introverted and didn't talk unless something needed to be said. Liz lit up the room everywhere she went. She had a huge smile and was a heck of a power forward. Her dad, Pierre Turgeon, played in the NHL, which I imagine added some pressure for her, although she never talked about it. However, she did wear his signature jersey number—number 77—on the ice. She was fiercely competitive, talented, and found a way to do everything with a big smile on her face.

One of the high points of the trip was going to a snow park. We had so much fun sliding around on the kind of inner tubes you might find at a summer water park. I remember one time Liz and I went up the gondola with no inner tubes, thinking we could get them at the top, and when we got there we realized we should have brought our inner tubes with us. We didn't know what to do so we just went ahead and started sliding down a giant mountain on our bellies. Well, ski patrol was not happy with us. They were yelling at us in French, which Liz knew but I didn't, so we laughed and just kept sliding down. It was definitely one of the best times I had—getting into low-key trouble, of course.

It was good we were able to release some tension because Manon was an intense coach to play for. She had high expectations for our team, and while so much of this tournament was about the experience, for Manon it was also about changing the narrative she'd been trying to change her whole life, now with the next generation. She felt it was important that people saw girls and women *do* belong in hockey. As a player, Manon had broken so many barriers, but now as a coach, she'd brought an all-American girls' team to the tournament for the first time. And she'd done it less than ten minutes away from her hometown. It was different, it was change, and it was controversial. She shouldered that pressure, protected us from the negativity, and pushed us to be our best because she knew we were proving so many people wrong at the same time we thought we were just playing in a hockey tournament.

She couldn't shield us from the pennies, but she did a darn good job keeping the other noise out. And in the process Manon challenged our potential. She had a lot of patience and relentlessly encouraged us to go outside our comfort zones because she knew better than all of us the challenges we would face ahead if we wanted to pursue careers in hockey, and especially what we would face as women if we remained on our paths.

I loved being at the Quebec International Pee-Wee Tournament. It was the perfect opportunity for me and every girl like me who had a dream to reach the pinnacle of the sport. Seeing girls who also played boys' hockey gave me the confidence to remind myself that I *did* belong. Making it to the semi-final at the tournament helped too. When I returned from Quebec, all of my Chicago Chill teammates were so jealous they hadn't gotten to go. While I felt bad, I was also proud I had earned my way to the tournament and been on a team made up of a lot of the best American girl players around my age. And since I'd played with girls who were a year older than me, I was eligible to return to the peewee tournament the following year. However, the following year when I was in seventh grade, Manon had to break the news to us that the peewee tournament officials were not allowing us back in the tournament because . . . we were girls.

CHAPTER 11

BIG DECISIONS: GIRLS' VS. BOYS' HOCKEY

When you feel like you've run into a brick wall, find a way to climb over it.

After two weeks in Quebec City, my teammates and I returned to our boys' teams. I was in sixth grade and in my third year of AAA hockey. The boys were starting to get much bigger than me, and as the season began to wind down, that became an issue because when I was a kid, body checking was allowed in peewees. I was playing full-check hockey, which meant if I had the puck, I was fair game. Anyone could use physical force to hurl me into the boards or launch me into open ice. Coaches are always preaching to keep your head up when you have the puck on your stick because you need to be ready to make a play, and there's also a better chance of avoiding a hit coming your way if you're alert, whereas if you have the puck on your stick with your head down, you won't be able to make a play and you'll for sure get hit. I've always been a small player, even among girls, and now that the boys were starting to go through puberty, the overall size difference was more obvious, so my family and I decided—along with Manon's recommendation—that this would be my last year playing boys' AAA hockey.

When the season ended, we also received news that the Chicago Chill AAA Hockey Club was folding. The hockey club that had meant so much to me was gone. Even though I recently made the decision to play girls' hockey after this season, I was heartbroken because I had been hoping to continue developing my skills by practicing with many of the same Chicago Chill '92 AAA teammates. I am so grateful for all the coaches and teammates, especially Coach Larry, who valued me as a hockey player and person from the very beginning. In our final season, we played more than one hundred games. I grew so much as a player but more importantly as a person.

While I had considered Manon to be my temporary coach during the peewee tournament, it turned out that was only the beginning of our relationship. With little to no opportunities at this point, my parents leaned on Manon for advice during this pivotal moment in my young hockey career. Manon recommended to my parents and me that I play part-time girls' hockey and practice with a AAA boys' team. I didn't love the idea at first because at the time the speed, skill, and overall pace of the girls' game was much slower than the boys'. I'd worked so hard to earn my skill set and I thought playing girls' hockey would not be challenging enough. I had just played with the best girls from all over the United States at the peewee tournament, and all of us went back to boys' teams for a reason.

So when it came to figuring out where to play next, we looked to Manon. She was living in Wisconsin at the time, which in hockey miles is not very far from Illinois. She was coaching a U12 (under twelve) girls' team called the Wisconsin Wild. Because of the trust we had in Manon, I decided to play there, but I still had to figure out what local boys' team I could practice with since the Chicago Chill dismantled. Thankfully, the Chicago Mission '92 boys' team welcomed me with open arms, letting me play a few games and practice with them. The team practiced three times a week, fifty minutes away from my house in Addison, Illinois. As for the Wisconsin Wild, I wasn't alone in this part-time setup. Five of us on the Wild played on boys' teams part-time in other states. We made the trek to Manon and the Wisconsin Wild because we were good players who didn't have adequate opportunities locally. Manon understood the challenges we faced and supported us.

My teammates on the Wild included fellow Olympic gold medalist Alex (Rigsby) Cavallini and Jordan (Slavin) Smith, who I played with in Quebec and later on Team USA. Even though we weren't together regularly, we worked well together. Our team was so good that we won the Wisconsin State Championship and went on to take second place at the USA Hockey National Championship tournament, losing in three overtimes in the final. Only the best teams in the United States make it to the USA Hockey National Championship, so that was an accomplishment I was really proud of. That year the national championships were held in Centennial, Colorado, which was home to Jordan. Mom and I stayed at her house, and it was almost more fun than the hockey itself. Her family had four-wheelers, an arcade, and a puck-shooting room, so we would bounce from one activity to the next. One time when we were on her family's farm, I lost control of the four-wheeler and crashed into a trailer that had a drag racing car inside of it. I put a hole in the trailer but thankfully missed the drag racing car . . . Oh, and I was okay too. Jordan is still one of my good friends to this day.

While I enjoyed all the winning and scoring I did with the Wisconsin Wild, I always remember how hard practice was with the Chicago Mission. Coach Pete would have us do ten "Herbies" (named after legendary coach Herb Brooks) at the end of practice. That meant goal line to near blue line and back, goal line to red line and back, goal line to far blue line and back, goal line to goal line and back, and that was *one*! My legs were numb by the end. These practices were very humbling. On the ice with the girls, I dominated, whereas when I was on the ice with the boys, I wasn't the best. It turned out those failures were what kept me driven and motivated. There was a lot of adjusting needed that year, but I realized this was what I had to do if I wanted to keep developing at my current pace. Trust me, this wasn't easy. Each week, I listened to the boys talk about how much fun they had at their most recent games, and saw the excitement they had preparing for upcoming opponents while I was just there to practice. Since I only played games with the Wisconsin Wild on sporadic weekends, I missed the team's daily camaraderie. I really didn't feel fully connected to either team.

As the season neared its end, the Chicago Mission '92s went to the same peewee tournament I'd gone to the year before. I skated alongside them as they prepared, reminded my Powerade team was not allowed back because we were girls. Right before they departed, our Mission coach, Tim Breslin, unexpectedly passed away. Coach Breslin would never want the team to miss out on the tournament, so they went on to Quebec City and I attended Coach Breslin's services without them. That was extremely difficult.

After the season ended, Manon moved to Michigan, which again is close in hockey miles, but her move meant the Wisconsin Wild was no longer an option. Once again, my parents leaned on Manon for advice. Manon said I could play part-time on her new team in Michigan as long as I could continue to practice with the Chicago Mission AAA boys' team. All my parents wanted was for me to feel supported in my growth as a person and player. I committed to playing part-time with the Michigan Icebreakers U16 girls' team as an eighth grader. This meant I was playing with girls who were three years older than me. It was an adjustment, but I was excited to meet all my new teammates and the new coach who would be coaching with Manon. His name was Tom Anastos. Coming from U12s with Manon the year before, playing U16s was a big jump. The players were much older than me, in high school, and some even had significant others.

Now that we were teenagers and professionalism was more important, Manon required us to dress up in khaki pants and a polo when we went to games. I'd never experienced that before. I was used to wearing tracksuits to games and wearing whatever I felt like the rest of the time. When I got to my first game, one of my teammates asked if I had the proper dress clothes and I was totally taken off guard and unprepared. We had to run to the mall to get overpriced khakis. I was so uncomfortable because they were so tight. Manon also would send workout plans, and I would print them off and do them by myself in my basement. A lot of them were bodyweight workouts—things like lunges, push-ups, box jumps (or coffee table jumps), sprints, and other things. This was really my first introduction to working out.

Our team had average talent with above-average coaches,

which was lucky for us because we learned so much and only got better every game. When it came time for the state tournament—which was a big deal because you need to win the Michigan state championship in order to go to the USA Hockey National Championship—we were the least-talented team in the state. All of the other teams were filled with players who were committed to play college hockey and our team was filled with players who didn't make those teams, so when we won the state tournament it was a big deal. It was *the* underdog story. We headed to Buffalo, New York, for the USA Hockey National Championship and we were the team representing our Michigan district at the U16 level. Our team made it to the quarterfinals. Although we did not win, it was an experience of a lifetime, a first and last for many of the players.

The underdog team winning the Michigan state tournament didn't sit well with some of the people in charge, however, so they took a closer look at who was on it. The Michigan Amateur Hockey Association (MAHA) officials considered me an outsider since I was from another state—and, disappointed none of their top teams made the national tournament, were convinced that I, as an eighth grader, was the cause of their problems. So when I tried to play for Manon and the Michigan Icebreakers for a second year in a row, MAHA invented "the Kendall Coyne rule," which stated that all players had to live within forty miles of the Michigan border. My coaches were quick to point out that I did. I lived within thirty-three miles as the crow flies. But then MAHA interpreted the rule saying it couldn't be as the crow flies and instead had to be assessed via driving miles. By that measurement, I lived too far away by three miles.

First, I was furious, then devastated. I had been cut from one team because I was a girl and disallowed from playing in the Quebec peewee tournament also because I was a girl, then I couldn't play with the boys because of the risk factors, and now I wasn't able to continue to learn from my mentor based on a made-up technicality. Everywhere I turned, I was told I didn't belong.

My parents and I had to go back to the drawing board. We looked at the options in Illinois, but the coaching was nowhere near what Manon and Coach Tom had to offer at the time. I had to do something, though; I couldn't just sit around waiting for my dream to fall into my lap. It turned out the last tryout for one of two girls' teams in Illinois was happening on the exact day MAHA rejected me. With it being so last minute, Mom and Dad were both tied up with Jake and Bailey, so Kevin drove me. I tried out for the Team Illinois U14 girls, because Team Illinois only allowed players to play at their age level. I made the team but was disappointed because I had played at the U16 level for Manon as a thirteen-year-old, successfully winning the state championship and going to the national tournament, and now I had to play at the U14 level. It felt like it could be a step back once again. But I knew I needed to play, and if this was my only option, I would take it, just like when I got cut from the AA team and my only option was house league. However, my decision to play girls' U14 did not come without first confirming I could continue to practice with the Chicago Mission '92 boys' team again. Thankfully they let me, but it was awkward at times because the Team Illinois AAA Hockey Club and the Chicago Mission AAA Hockey Club are archrivals in Illinois AAA youth hockey. It would be like the Chicago White Sox versus the Chicago Cubs (go White Sox), and I was on both teams!

I am so glad I had the support of both clubs. On many nights, Mom would drive me to Addison to practice with the Chicago Mission boys, and then after practice we would scoot twenty minutes away to a different rink, where my Team Illinois practice would be taking place. It was crazy, but I loved being on the ice.

That year we won the Illinois State Championship and went on to win the USA Hockey National Championship in San Jose, California, as the best team in the country at the U14 level. So while MAHA thought they could get rid of me by inventing a rule to prevent me from playing, I ended up getting the last word, beating a team from Michigan for the national championship. I was proud to be on top, to win; and at fourteen years old I had already won three state championships in three different states and played in three national championships—medaling in two of them. In my mind, the Olympic dream was once again alive and achievable . . . yet it had been years since 2002 when I saw the Women's National Team play, because none of the games were ever televised. And at this point I had yet to see a women's college hockey game.

But even with those victories, the first few years of girls' hockey were heavy. I kept having to reposition myself and reconsider how I was going to achieve my dreams. I was constantly questioning if I was doing enough, pushing myself hard enough. Not having consistency with my teams, coaches, and schedule in girls' hockey was difficult. Pressures were coming at me from all angles and I often wished things would go a different way. I felt in my gut that all these things were happening to me because I was too good, and there was nowhere for me to go. I was upsetting the status quo, shaking up the way things had always been done, and there were lots of people who didn't like that and wanted to keep me in my lane. That's just not how I'm built. I will always rise up and give my best, and I'm always looking for the next means of bettering myself. That year, however, it was like running an obstacle course with brick walls in the middle of each path. People kept standing in my way, making things harder, and it was fatiguing.

GOLDEN COYNE

Find a mentor who really cares about you and sees your potential before you see it yourself. Mentors won't always tell you what you want to hear—be a great listener, knowing they have your best interest in mind.

As upset as I got over all the things that happened that year, they forced me to refocus on what I wanted to achieve and what I ultimately wanted, period. Manon's advice was vital for me in many ways, and I'm thankful our relationship has continued to this day. Being coached by her and playing on all-girls teams opened my eyes to the fact that even though space for women in hockey was limited, I could create a place for myself and others like me. And that there *were* other girls who loved hockey as much as me and worked as hard. So when I got knocked down, I kept getting back up. I kept winning, even if the wins were hard to find. And the thing is, if I had taken any of those negative experiences as defeats or reflections of my capabilities, I would have quit. That would have been way easier. But then again, if I had done that, I never would have experienced what came next.

CHAPTER 12

OPPORTUNITIES WITHIN REACH

Sometimes your biggest opportunities are the ones you create for yourself.

After three wonderful years at Palos South Middle School, the mild-mannered caterpillars that had once filled my stomach were now full-fledged butterflies because I was getting ready to start high school. Our high school district has three schools within it. Kevin attended Amos Alonzo Stagg High School, which was where the majority of our friends from middle school attended. During Kevin's freshman year, there were several problems within Stagg, so when it came time for me (and later Jake and Bailey) to make the jump to high school, my parents were concerned and asked for a principal's transfer to one of the other two schools in the district, Carl Sandburg High School.

Sandburg is a public school in Orland Park with four thousand students—and if my principal's transfer was approved, I would be meeting mostly all-new students as well as all-new teachers, so I would be overwhelmed. And Kevin would still be at Stagg, meaning I'd have no older brother support either.

My principal's transfer was approved, but because of a paperwork delay, I found out I would be going to Carl Sandburg High School a day too late . . .

I missed the first day of high school.

I know. It was one day. But here's the thing: when I am under competitive pressure, I flip a switch, beast mode kicks in, and I find a way to be the best version of myself. On the other hand, when I have to figure out who I'm going to sit with in a high school lunchroom, I crumble and become a very introverted and shy person. Also, it's amazing how fast the social order organizes itself, so you'd think one day is no big deal, but actually it was like I had missed everything.

When Mom dropped me off at Sandburg for the first time, I didn't walk in through the same doors as all the other students. I used the guest entrance, signed my name on a pad of paper, and was given a hall pass with strict orders to go directly to the guidance office, a relatively long walk through the lunchroom.

Earlier in the summer, every incoming freshman had visited Sandburg for orientation. They were given school IDs, received bus assignments, and picked up their class schedules. Since the principal's transfer had not yet been finalized, I had missed orientation. I felt lost as I watched kids zoom past me, assured and confident.

All I remember is one foot after the next getting me closer to the guidance office door, where I was hoping I could hide for the rest of the day. I met my guidance counselor, Mrs. Blaschek, for the first time, who was there to help. She asked me if I knew anyone,

anyone at all in the building. When I told her there was only one person, Mackenzie Nagle, she sighed with relief. Mackenzie's dad and my dad grew up together, therefore so did we; in fact, we were born one month apart! Mrs. Blaschek scrapped my whole schedule and gave us the same lunch period. *Phew*. One butterfly off on its merry way.

At the time I entered high school, the Blackhawks had just drafted Jonathan Toews followed by Patrick Kane. These two stars led the Blackhawks to a resurgence, and the increasing wins coupled with their games now being televised meant hockey was the talk of the town, which transmitted into the overall growth of the game. Parents flocked to rinks for Learn to Play Hockey classes and to get their kids on teams. Blackhawks tickets were now hard to come by. People were suddenly loving the sport that had seemed invisible to everyone outside of my inner circle my whole life. The Blackhawks' successes had a direct impact in my hockey world too.

Because of the increased participation in youth hockey in Illinois, the Chicago Mission decided to start a girls' hockey club. After playing U14s as a freshman and winning a national championship, I was ready for a new challenge. I was thrilled to join the new girls' organization and help build something special. Most girls' programs have four age levels—U12, U14, U16, and U19—but because the Mission's program was new, there weren't enough players to fill all those teams yet. So we started with just two teams, U14 and U19, with me on the U19. Doing so also meant I would get to play against girls older than me again, just like when I was on the Michigan Icebreakers U16 team.

Before the social media era, I would spend half my lunch eating with Mackenzie and the other half catching up on homework in the computer lab. If I had free time, I would then scroll through websites for any information I could get having to do with hockey. One day I was on the USA Hockey website and saw a press release from the International Ice Hockey Federation (IIHF) announcing the launch of the IIHF Under-18 Women's World Championship. The first-of-its-kind women's tournament would be comprised of eight countries, including the United States. Up to this point, I'd had no idea where to find opportunities to represent my country in hockey or if I was even able to play on a US team yet, but as I read the release I realized as a '92 birth year, and fifteen years old, I was eligible for this event. How was I going to get there? Well, that part wasn't on the press release, but with a pep in my step as I went through the rest of my classes that day, I couldn't wait to get home from school and tell my parents about what I'd discovered.

Shortly after the press release, USA Hockey announced that Katey Stone, the head coach of Harvard's women's hockey team, would be the first head coach of the US Under-18 Women's National Team. Since I didn't know how to try out for the team, I immediately went to the women's hockey section on Harvard's website and found Coach Stone's contact information. The only problem was, *I* didn't have an email address. I'm pretty sure I created the one I still use to this day just to write Coach Stone to ask her how to try out for the team. It seems so brave now, but I just thought, *This is something I want*, and I went for it. When I got home from school, I told my parents about my intentions and broke the news I had already asked her how to make the team.

This was my dream. I needed to know how to get there.

Coach Stone wrote me back.

She told me that the process would begin by picking a U18 Women's National Select Team after evaluating all Player Development Camps that summer. The players chosen for the U18 Women's *Select* Team would then go on to the USA Hockey Women's National August Festival and compete in a three-game series against Team Canada. This would give the coaching staff another opportunity to evaluate the players prior to selecting a *National Team* that would play in the inaugural U18 Women's World Championships five months later in January of 2008.

I had some familiarity with the player development camps because I attended the U14 one in Rochester, New York, one year prior. At this time, player development camps were broken down into four age groups: U14, U15, U16, and U17. The process to be invited to a player development camp starts with your district. There are twelve districts within USA Hockey, and each district has a certain number of players they can invite to the player development camp based on the amount of registered hockey players in that area. For example, states like Minnesota and Michigan are their own districts because of their large number of registered hockey players, but states with smaller hockey numbers—like Illinois—are combined to create a wider-ranging district. After my district conducted tryouts, I was selected to attend the U15 player development camp. With only one hundred players being invited in total per age group, you needed to be one of the top one hundred girls of your age bracket.

After the U15, U16, and U17 player development camps ended (the three eligible birth years for the U18 team), Coach Stone and the selection committee would need to pick twenty-two players to make up the 2007 U18 Women's Select National Team, which would go on to the USA Hockey Women's National August Festival to prepare to play Team Canada in that three-game series I mentioned earlier. So when you really break it down, the evaluators had to get from three hundred to twenty-two after scouting all three of the player development camps.

From that point forward, I ramped up my training so I could become one of those twenty-two. I had stopped playing travel softball with the Oak Lawn Ice and stuck to high school softball during the academic year, so I had the time and space to really focus. And down in my basement, I continued to do the workouts Manon had once sent me. I knew putting in the work to make the U18 National Team would bring me one step closer to my ultimate goal of becoming an Olympian.

I was excited to face my new challenges and meet all the new players from around the United States at the U15 Player Development Camp in St. Cloud, Minnesota, many of whom I had never seen play. In some ways it was similar to playing in the International Pee-Wee Hockey Tournament while being coached by Manon, in that it was inspiring, intimidating, and a huge dream come true. I was getting to compete with and against the best U15 girls in the country.

I was excited even though getting to know those players was sometimes overwhelming because of my introverted nature. The upside was, no matter who I sat with at lunch, I knew we had common interests that helped start a conversation. Most of these girls loved the game as much as I did and had the same dreams of making the inaugural U18 team and one day playing in the Olympics.

After the week-long camp I headed home and waited to hear my fate. All the other player developments had concluded. The

U15 one was the last, so the final decisions were being made. A couple of days later I got an email from the Women's National Team general manager, Michele Amidon. I remember the moment clear as day. I was lying on Bailey's bed because I was too tired from camp to climb to my top bunk when Mom woke me up to tell me I had an email from USA Hockey. I leaped up, clanked my head on the bunk bed, ran downstairs to our family computer, and opened the email I knew would determine my fate.

I had made the team.

I felt very fortunate to be eligible for the first ever U18 Women's National Select Team, just like I had been on the first all-girls team in the Quebec tournament. So many incredible players who came before me didn't have these opportunities.

And while I was fortunate, what might have happened if I'd been too afraid to send an email to Coach Stone? Would I have missed out on the U18 team completely had I not been looking for every opportunity to get better at the game? What if I had become complacent and didn't continue to practice with the AAA boys' teams when I started playing girls' hockey, or I hadn't been surrounded by the best coaches at that level because my parents didn't want to put up with the hassles it took to join those teams? What would have happened if I'd stopped pushing myself all the time and lost my determination to be the best player and teammate I could be?

Thankfully, I (and my parents) had put in the work so I could position myself to achieve my goals, instead of looking back with regrets that I could have done more.

I tell people all the time, follow your dreams and goals and be willing to put in the work it takes to accomplish those dreams and goals. Whether it was my email to Coach Stone, my performance at the player development camp, the training I did in my basement leading up to the National Camp, practicing with boys and girls, or a combination of all the above, accomplishing my goal of making the U18 Women's National Select Team was the beginning of everything for me.

Everything.

GOLDEN COYNE

It is easy to focus on the things you are good at. But if you want to push yourself beyond your limits, get comfortable being uncomfortable. Identify your strengths and your weaknesses, then work hard to turn your weaknesses into strengths. Create a quality plan and write down the action steps you will take to get there. If there's a will, there's a way.

CHAPTER 13

NO EQUIPMENT,
NO PROBLEM

*The decisions you make will either
support your goals or obstruct them.*

The 2007 USA Hockey Women's National August Festival was
held in Lake Placid, New York. I was aware of the historical
significance of the location. The Miracle on Ice, as we know it
today, took place there. In 1980, in the midst of the Cold War, the
young underdogs from the United States beat the heavily favored
Soviets, who had won the last four consecutive gold medals at the
Olympic games. The world had said it couldn't be done, and as
the clock hit zero, famous broadcaster Al Michaels said, "Do you
believe in miracles. . . . YES!" While I wasn't alive to witness the
game in real time, this is a staple moment in sports history, hockey
history, and USA Hockey history.

And now there I was, twenty-seven years after the Miracle on
Ice, fifteen years old and the youngest player to be at the Women's
National Team August Festival, about to put on my first Team USA

jersey. I would be playing with the best of the best. There would be a U18 team (my team), a U22 team, and the Women's National Team all under the same roof. I was ready for the challenge.

Aaaaannd I was late.

The problem was my parents and I hadn't booked the flight and weren't used to flying out of Chicago's O'Hare airport. Unfortunately, new regulations had been put into place since 9/11 and because of them United Airlines wouldn't let me check my bags since we had arrived less than an hour prior to the departure time, so Mom had to send my sticks and hockey bag via UPS. You can probably imagine how much I was stressing, taking off for the most important camp of my life without any equipment. The entire flight into Albany, New York, all I thought about was my bags that were missing from the cargo.

My late arrival was also partly because no one had expected me or any other fifteen-year-old to be selected from the U15 player development camp that was held the week before the start of the August Festival—as a result, I'd been a last-minute addition. This also meant that on top of being the youngest player on the team, I was the least known.

When I got into Lake Placid, my new teammates were already in the weight room warming up for on-ice fitness testing, so I had to hurry up to join them, but wasn't sure what would come next—as I didn't have my gear. Of course, this being the most intense and elite training camp on planet earth, there were no excuses, and I wasn't about to make any. I had to find a way to deal with my situation. Borrowing equipment was an obvious solution, but as usual I was the smallest player on the team. I've never apologized for it, but my size has always been something I've needed to contend with.

When I walked into the rink, I was greeted by an equipment manager, who gave me a T-shirt and shorts and said, "Hey, kid, I heard about your equipment snafu—we are working on getting equipment for you so you can test today." I quietly nodded my head and said thank you. I'd never had an equipment manager before. There were so many staff members there: coaches, nutritionists, athletic trainers, doctors, equipment managers, a massage therapist, a mental skills coach, and more. It was overwhelming at first but a real eye-opener, because they were all there to help us get better and be the best in the world, and they were the best in the world at what they did.

The equipment manager pointed to the locker room the U18 team was in, and I hurried to change into my new workout clothes so I could join the warm-up with my teammates. When I entered the locker room, everyone had a stall with their name and number and their equipment hanging below. I didn't have a stall with my name and number, and of course I didn't have equipment. Nervous I didn't belong in there, I popped back into the hallway to find the equipment manager. He reassured me that it was the U18 locker room, and I told him I didn't have a stall. They had forgotten. When I did get one, my name was spelled wrong: Kendal, missing the second *L*.

Again, I was determined not to make any excuses or to ask for any special treatment, but the fact remained that I didn't have any equipment and the on-ice conditioning test was about to start. As a solution, our equipment manager found the next-smallest player, who was in her first year of college and on the U22 team, and asked her to loan me some gear. Who would have thought my experience wearing Rocco's equipment when I was eleven years old would prepare me for this moment?

However, her equipment didn't fit quite like Rocco's. She was a little bit bigger than me, maybe 5 foot two, 125 pounds, while I was 5 feet and 105 pounds at the most. Her gear was also top of the line. Everything was fancy and new, and nothing was very broken in. This spelled disaster for me. As I've mentioned before, all my stuff was secondhand, old, falling apart, barely even protective, and that was how I liked it. This was like wearing brand-new shoes that were two sizes too big and then being asked to run the biggest race of your life in them! *Good luck!* I felt completely stiff and out of place. The other personal stressor I had walking into Lake Placid was figuring out who was going to braid my hair. Mom wouldn't be there. My hair had to be in a braid every day. Thankfully, Anne (Schleper) Span was a kind soul and sensed my panic and asked if I needed something. I wanted to start with my hockey equipment, but I asked her if she knew how to braid. She responded with excitement, "Yes!" and my first friend and hair braider on the team was established.

My teammate's skates felt huge, and as it turned out so was her helmet . . . it fell off my head mid-test. One coach grabbed the helmet and chased me down the ice. He told me to stop and put it back on, but with no time to respond I sped up because I wanted to complete the test as fast as I could. I kept going. I had to. I got through all the fitness tests. I completed each one the best I could.

GOLDEN COYNE

Control what you can control: your work ethic, your attitude, how you handle adversity, and your personal drive. It's the only way to get better in whatever you want to succeed in.

Meanwhile, I was completely fascinated by what I was observing around me. This was a level of athleticism I had never witnessed before. The care these athletes had when it came to their routines, bodies, and workouts inspired me and made me realize I had miles to go before I reached their level. Honestly, I had never thought very deeply about nutrition and recovery before. Yes, I had given up pop and had made a connection that junk food wasn't the way to be a top athlete, but this was entirely different. All around me, people were drinking smoothies, taking ice baths, cooling down after workouts, foam rolling their muscles, and going to bed early. I realized they weren't athletes just while they were working out or playing; they were athletes all the time, every moment of every day. The Olympics may only be every four years, but the path to get there is paved with relentless effort every day. I recognized that if I wanted to be as good as them and keep my place in the game, I would have to incorporate more of what they were doing.

At the end of the camp we traveled to Ottawa, Ontario, for a three-game series against Team Canada's U18 Select team—this time my equipment arrived right on time.

Well, we lost all three games.

We not only lost, we got smoked. I realized how much more difficult it was to be successful at this level. The games were harder and faster, everyone was strong and skilled. Our bodies got beat up, and because of that our athletic trainer required us to take ice baths after our games, two at a time inside a giant garbage can. I was paired up with defenseman Sasha Sherry, who was six feet tall compared to my five feet. I got in first. It was *horrible*. When Sasha got in, the water rose even higher than it already was, and the extreme rise made me puke everywhere. Let's just say it's rare to find me in a cold tub these days.

At the end of the two weeks together, we received our evaluations. Out of all the U18 forwards, I was ranked number 1, which surprised me considering my age. In addition to the position ranking, we were ranked on a Likert scale from excellent to poor in the character traits we possessed as hockey players, such as speed, skill, shot, hockey sense, compete level, strength, and other areas that USA Hockey felt were critical for a player to have success at this level. However, there was one category that really humbled me: the mark next to strength was *Poor*. I had never received a grade this *poor* before in anything, and it shook me; that one mark has affected how I approach everything I do even to this day. I was determined to never be called out for lack of strength again. The conversation with myself went like this: "There's no reason you can't be the strongest player on the team; if you commit to being the strongest player, you can be and you will be. Why shouldn't you be? Because you're small? That may be an excuse for others, but it won't be for you."

I decided I needed to increase my training off the ice. Being fifteen years old, I wasn't lifting as much as the older players; I was doing the predominately bodyweight workouts in my basement that Manon had sent me, but that was about to change. After getting swept in the three-game series, none of us knew if we would get called back to be members of the U18 Women's National Team to compete in the U18 Women's World Championships. The combination of getting swept by Team Canada and my evaluation motivated me, and I went home determined to be the strongest and the hardest-working. I was going to become better, no matter what it took.

CHAPTER 14

ANN ARBOR

Be a sponge: listen, learn, and observe.

As I was waiting to hear my fate with the U18 Team, I was invited to Ann Arbor, Michigan, that October to train with the Senior Women's National Team. This training camp was utilized to prepare for the Four Nations Cup, a tournament between rival countries the United States, Finland, Sweden, and Canada.

Since some of the Women's National Team players who'd be attending the Four Nations Cup were in college, USA Hockey didn't want them missing an extra week of classes on top of the week they would miss for the tournament, so instead they took the high school–aged players out of school so they could join the postgraduate players for just the week of training camp. I was more than happy to fill a hole, as it was another opportunity to learn and be surrounded by my idols.

I was also starting to realize my success wasn't a fluke. I was one of only six U18 players in the country who had been chosen to fill in at this camp. That meant I had the potential to get to the senior national team level if I stayed the course.

I was fascinated by the veteran players, watching them for hints that would help me become more like them. I was determined to figure out how they got to where I want to be. One day we all went to Potbelly's for dinner, and I ordered the exact same meal as Natalie Darwitz, one of the best players ever to play the game, thinking maybe that was the key. I'm kidding about believing that was her secret, but it shows how far I was willing to go to glean some idea of what it took. I was in awe of her and everyone else who was there.

At the same time, I was reckoning with the intersection between my shortcomings and my ambitions. I was fifteen years old, competing with Jenny Potter (Pottsey), who at twenty-eight was one of the oldest players. I didn't have nearly the experience that was needed to keep up with these stars in the weight room, and the training sessions in Ann Arbor were extremely strenuous. At one point, the strength coach told us to go get our skates and skate guards and wear them in the weight room (this is not normal; skates are meant for ice). We stood in our skates in a circle and passed a forty-five-pound plate over our heads. Captain and leader Julie Chu (aka Chuey) was to the right of me. I watched the plate go from player to player with ease. Too much ease, like they did this in their sleep. As the plate got closer, I knew it was too heavy to hold over my head. At that point, there was nothing I could do and I was honestly just going to let it crush me. When the plate came to me, my arms started to cave, the plate began to dip, and Chuey grabbed it just before it crushed my head. She *almost* let me fail but helped me enough to let me know she had my back. I knew the onus was then on me to make sure I could do the exercise. At the same time, I was embarrassed she needed to help me, mortified I wasn't as strong as the other players. My inability to hold the forty-five-pound plate over my head shows I deserved the poor grade I received in the strength category of my evaluation at the August Festival. In team sports, you're as strong as your weakest link, and because I wasn't strong, it felt like I was letting the team down.

GOLDEN COYNE

Confidence comes from preparation. If you put in the work it takes to be prepared, you will be ready to meet any challenge head-on knowing you have done everything in your control.

Regardless of mood, exhaustion, personal issues, or whatever we had going on in our lives, we were expected to set those aside and be all in while we were training, sometimes even with injuries. One of the other six U18 players at the camp stepped on a puck and twisted her ankle during practice. When she came back after being sent to get X-rays, we were in the midst of a workout. She had crutches and a soft cast on her ankle, so we knew it must not have been good news. Instead of asking how she was feeling or showing any compassion, our strength coach, Teena Murray, looked her up and down and said, "Why aren't you ready to work out?"

My teammate looked down at her newly casted ankle and said, "I'm injured."

The strength coach said, "Yeah, well, you have another leg. Let's go."

It was one of those moments where you realize that sort of thing isn't just in the movies. It really is the expectation.

That was just how it was.

We also did a body fat test, a first for me. When they pulled out the calipers, I was like, *What are those?* Pottsey, who had her second baby nine months earlier, had a body fat percentage that was lower than mine. I was blown away!

Yes, I was more connected to my physical body than the average fifteen-year-old, but I was nowhere near these women, who had made optimizing themselves for the game their central purpose and pursuit. It was a huge wake-up call, and I was there to watch and learn from all of them.

Once my week filling in at the camp was over and I got settled back in at home, I was all over my mom to find me a strength coach, but I knew my parents didn't have extra money. I was always very aware of that fact and didn't want to put pressure on them or stress them out in that way, but I also knew that my development had come to a point where if I didn't take action, I would be putting myself at a serious disadvantage. The basement workouts weren't going to cut it anymore.

Mom understood, and after she did some budgeting she figured out that they could afford six weeks of training. She went straight for the best and approached Paul Goodman, the strength and conditioning coach for the Chicago Blackhawks. I appreciated Mom's mindset so much on this move. She knew we could only afford a few weeks, so she sought out someone local who could provide me with the best foundation in a short amount of time.

Paul had just begun his first year with the Blackhawks. He was somehow okay with waking up at four in the morning a couple of times a week to give me invaluable foundational information about how to lift weights safely, how to get stronger, how to stay healthy, and how to build myself up so I could be the best possible athlete on and off the ice. I took that information and worked tirelessly to integrate it into my life. I was extremely lucky that Paul understood what my mom had told him about our finances and my needs—that I had come back from my time with the Women's National Team realizing I had potential but needed to get stronger to compete at the highest level.

While I was reflecting on the commitment I saw from the players I was just surrounded by, I remembered a nutrition lecture I attended in Lake Placid. It had deeply affected me because I noticed that the players lived by everything the nutritionist preached. When I got home from Ann Arbor, I told Mom she had to get rid of the white bread and the whole milk, among many other things. She handled it all with her usual salty good humor and made the adjustments, but for me it was transformational.

Everything was amplified and taken to the next level as I continued having success. After Ann Arbor, I was required to register with the United States Anti-Doping Agency (USADA), who ensures Team USA athletes are competing clean. I had to submit my whereabouts, which meant a sixty-minute time window of where I would be every day so they knew where to find me within that period. They would randomly show up, and I was always so worried they would show up at Sandburg and embarrass me by having me pee in a cup in front of a witness. Once, I was at the rink for practice and had to ask a teammate's mom to chaperone me through the process, since I was still under eighteen. It was awkward!

That's all to say, everything was now at the next level, even the sacrifices I had to make.

Meanwhile, I was still in my first year with the Chicago Mission U19 girls' team and practicing with the U18 boys' team multiple days a week; I was at the rink for six-plus hours practicing with both teams. The U18 boys' practices were at 5:10 p.m. and the girls' practices started at 9:10 p.m., which meant they didn't end until 10:30 at night and really made for an early morning at school. In between the boys' practice and girls' practice, I would work out with my new foundation thanks to Paul, do my homework, and eat dinner. I was also committed to implementing my new learnings from Team USA such as foam rolling and drinking chocolate milk for recovery.

Oftentimes, I would be drinking that chocolate milk in the late-night car ride home with my teammate and friend, Amanda Boskovich (Bosko). She was a year older than me, had her driver's license, and lived on the southside like me, so she would offer to drive me home. Some say I learned how to drive from her . . .

All in all, these experiences grew my mindset in the sense I wasn't just thinking about how to be the best for my Chicago Mission teammates but for my new teammates on Team USA as well. I knew that if I made a bad decision, it would impact more than just me.

I strove for perfection and at times was obsessive, and as a result I approached everything with extreme care and attention to detail. I tried to improve every time I did something. That also meant I didn't allow myself to have much fun outside of the rink. I was serious about every aspect of what I was undertaking because I could feel that I was getting closer to my dream.

Maybe if I went back in time and loosened up a little, I wouldn't be where I am. It's hard to say. I like to think I had a pretty clear understanding of the world I was in and the reality of what I was facing: Nothing was going to be handed to me. I was going to have to earn every chance I got, so I'd better adapt and improve at every turn.

The good thing is, I learned what it meant to be elite at a young age. The bad thing, if there is one, is that I didn't have much balance, as everything I did was structured around earning the opportunity to play for Team USA.

There was nothing else that seemed as critically important in my life at that time.

Nothing but hockey.

CHAPTER 15

ON TOP OF THE WORLD

*Sometimes, the victory isn't about the
win, but what you choose to take
away from the experience.*

After the three-game series with Canada, I thought all that was left was the announcement of the U18 Women's National Team. Little did I know there would be yet another try-out held in December, in Lake Placid. I received an email from USA Hockey explaining that I had been invited to try out and was shocked to see only eleven members from the U18 National Select team who'd participated in the three-game series on the tryout roster. That sent a huge message. They were not happy with our three-game performance, were bringing in a slew of new players to this tryout, and would be picking a team of the best twenty-two players at the end of the week.

My trip to Lake Placid was much smoother this time. I got my equipment, I had a name tag with my name spelled right, and the number 11 was assigned to me. We had to do all of the same fitness tests again, we played inter-squad scrimmages, and after a week Coach Stone announced the team and by doing so sent the others home.

I made the team. I was so relieved. I was off to Calgary, Alberta, with twenty-one other players to represent Team USA. I was excited because I wasn't the only player from my '92 birth year anymore: Liz Turgeon—my friend from the peewee tournament in Quebec— and Meagan Mangene, who was from New York, had made Team USA's U18 National Team lineup as well.

On January 8, 2008, I made my international debut with the U18 Women's National Team with an 11–0 win against Team Russia. Not only was this a great start to the inaugural U18 tournament, our new team ended up going undefeated, also beating Sweden and Switzerland in the preliminary round and beating the Czech Republic in the semifinals, which led to us playing Team Canada. We beat them 5–2 in the gold medal game. I scored the third and game-winning goal. I didn't think anything of the goal in the moment, other than it helped us secure the win and a gold medal.

This win was the first time I understood what it felt like to earn the right to hear "The Star-Spangled Banner" played over the loudspeaker, locked arm in arm with my teammates as the American flag was raised higher than the second- and third-place teams'. This was our Stanley Cup moment. It's a feeling that's hard to describe, a crowning achievement that makes all the work and sacrifices worth it. It helped me to recognize that part of what I'd been trying to do for so many years was get to a place where I represented the United States of America at the pinnacle of my sport, alongside the best players in the world—just like Cammi.

But back to that third goal I didn't think anything of. Our equipment manager asked me to go into the hallway when I got a chance. Phil Pritchard from the Hockey Hall of Fame, who is most known as the Keeper of the Stanley Cup, was there. Everyone in the hockey world knows who he is. Well, when I stepped into the hallway, he politely asked for my stick for *the hall*! Let me clarify: Phil wanted *my stick* for the Hockey Hall of Fame because I scored the game-winning goal in the first-ever U18 Women's World Championship. At first, I was thrilled. I thought of the treasured red-and-blue trifold Velcro wallet that I'd gotten from the Hockey Hall of Fame when I was a kid. That place had been so cool. It was *still* so cool!

But then panic set in.

Hockey sticks are expensive. Mine was originally a one-piece stick, but I broke the blade before the tournament, so I needed to get a wood blade as a replacement to put into the other end opposed to replacing the entire stick. Wood blades were cheap, but getting a brand-new one-piece graphite stick was not, and Mom had searched all the pro shops in Chicago to find me the specific blade I wanted. I appreciated the great lengths she had gone to. Even though my stick was already broken once, old, and beat-up, I knew if Phil took my stick, my parents would have to buy me a new one, so I freaked out and told him I had to ask my parents first. (I wonder if that ever happened to him before.) I couldn't find my parents because they'd been sent back to the hotel to wait for us, and we didn't have a way to get ahold of each other. So, completely in panic, I gave the stick to Phil without asking.

After the game, we went to a gold medal reception at the hotel, where my parents waited with Liz's parents, the Turgeons. They'd befriended each other in Quebec and had stayed in touch. My parents were beyond excited to congratulate me for the win but could sense something was wrong when I wasn't jumping for joy. Mom asked if everything was okay. I explained I had given my hockey stick away. There was a pause.

"To the Hockey Hall of Fame," I said, looking down almost in tears.

That caught even Dad off guard, and I tried to explain.

Pierre Turgeon, Liz's dad—who had just finished his twenty-year career in the NHL—said, "It took me five hundred goals in the NHL for the Hockey Hall of Fame to ask for my stick. You made the right choice."

My parents weren't mad at all, of course. They couldn't have been prouder.

So that's how my beat-up, once-broken, old, worn-down hockey stick wound up in the Hockey Hall of Fame.

I view my stick in the Hall of Fame as an opportunity to highlight the women's game on a huge platform. Since 2008, the hundreds of thousands of people who have walked through the Hall of Fame have seen my stick and other moments from that tournament. They can now see how far women's hockey has come and how much talent is in the women's game. We work so hard every day and yet so many people have no idea when or where we play or

GOLDEN COYNE

In order to be your best, surround yourself with the best— because in order to be the best, you have to beat the best.

really how good we are. I know there are many young girls who walk into the Hockey Hall of Fame like I once did, but unlike when I was there, they see representation and opportunities. They know it could be them someday. They know they can be a part of history and play in that tournament too.

When I think back on that achievement, of course I think of the feeling of satisfaction, being at the top, and having a gold medal around my neck, which I had always wanted. At fifteen I had accomplished a childhood dream. But I also think about my parents and every step we took together as a family, because I know I didn't get there alone. Bigger victories were yet to come, but I celebrated that one like it would be my last. I had learned through the adversities I had faced up until this point in my career to never take the victories for granted. It is hard to be on top and even harder to stay on top. If it was easy, everyone would do it. There was more work to be done.

CHAPTER 16

MORE THAN A HOCKEY PLAYER

Balance, balance, balance.

I came back to school on an emotional high after winning the gold medal and making history. While most kids at school had no idea why I had missed another three weeks of school, they started to know me as the girl in the braid who was always gone for hockey. However, Mackenzie was aware of my accomplishment and was excited to celebrate—she had decorated my locker and brought balloons and a cookie cake that was red, white, and blue.

As I wrapped up my sophomore year of high school and my first year with the Chicago Mission U19 girls' team, my dream of playing Division I hockey was always in the back of my mind, and I knew my performance as an underaged player on Team USA as well as my performance with the Mission would attract attention from the college scouts. After all, my Chicago Mission team won a state championship, earned our way to the national championship tournament in West Chester, Pennsylvania, and won the whole thing! We were a brand-new girls' program in our first year, and we ended winning the USA Hockey National Tournament as the best U19 girls' team in the country. It was an incredible feat that really put the Chicago Mission Girls Hockey Club on the map. I was so proud to be part of it.

Oh, and bonus?

We beat a team representing the state of Michigan.

Just like I learned early on, actions continued to speak louder than words.

I also suited up for my final year of softball for Sandburg. Hockey was my sport, and it was time for it to have all my focus. Even though that focus needed some adjustments. After my first year donning the red, white, and blue, I realized I needed better balance in my life because I was starting to get injured. Since I was so stubborn and refused to slow down even for a second, I ignored the warning signs the first and second times I got hernias and was eventually forced to take a break.

Although I was strong and in peak physical condition in some respects, I was also on my third hernia surgery by sixteen. A hernia is a ball of intestine that splits a hole in your abdominal wall if it's in your stomach area, which mine were. Anytime you cough, move, poop, basically do anything that requires usage of your core—which is everything—it's painful. Sometimes while you have a hernia, you can see the bulge. When the bulge popped out, I would push it back through my abdominal wall. I know, gross. It also hurts. A lot. During player development camps, I made a joke out of it and would pull my T-shirt tightly against my stomach and show everyone the ball. We named it Hi-hi. The girls would say, "How's Hi-hi today?" I'd say, "She's good!"

Sports humor, amiright?

Of course, I wouldn't sit still for forty-eight hours and flat-out refused to get surgery. I told my parents there was no way I could do anything that would compromise my ability to participate in any hockey events. I could play hurt. I pushed through and exercised mind over matter . . . three times.

I was trying to play catch-up in the weight room with players who had ten or more years of experience. I didn't realize there was nothing to catch up to, that I had to give myself time to grow. I was so stubborn, I had ignored the doctor's orders to allow myself adequate recovery the first time and had started working out way too soon—even though I told my parents I wasn't—which had made my injuries even worse and led to my second and third surgeries. And after the last of those surgeries, I also ignored the nurse's order to lay in the hospital bed when left alone. When the nurse left, I saw it as an opportunity to sit up. As I did, I passed out, fell off the bed, broke my nose, cut my head open, and had to get twelve stitches. My gut was cut open, my head was cut open too, and my nose was crushed. It all complemented my dimple and the twenty-three stitches from that sharks and minnows game well. That's when I finally, *finally* realized I had to slow down and face the fact (pun intended) that I had pushed myself too hard.

Ya think, Kendall?

Balance is a part of being elite. I had to learn in my own way the difference between working hard and working smart.

At the start of my junior year, I was starting to figure out my physical balances. But I also had to figure out how to balance my life overall.

Junior year of high school means taking the ACT and SAT and

having conversations about college. Being a highly touted recruit, I started to realize I only had a couple of years to prove myself at the high school level, and the college coaches weren't just evaluating my hockey abilities; they were looking at my grades too.

I had missed fifty days of school during my sophomore year. Fifty.

I had a gold medal win under my belt, which was huge, but my high school experience was completely abnormal. And for a long time, I didn't mind. I'd never fully had a regular school experience because my focus had always been elsewhere, but it was too extreme during my sophomore year. I realized that even though I had an excellent work ethic and tendency to be super detail-oriented, I had let my grades slip below my standards (okay, so it was Bs, but still). I was out of touch with everything besides hockey.

School became the balance I needed. I started to put the same energy into school as I did into hockey. I got really good at forging relationships with teachers. My junior year I had an English teacher, Mr. Maguire, who didn't let me fade into the background. Even though I still didn't speak up much in his class, it was always the one I felt the most comfortable in because of a poster he had hanging on the wall. The words still sit with me to this day. It said, "Thirty years from now, it won't matter what shoes you wore, how your hair looked, or the jeans you bought. What will matter is what you learned and how you used it." For someone who wore her hair in a braid every single day and got made fun of for it, never wore jeans, and always wore gym shoes and athletic clothes, you can see how this one little poster spoke to me every day I sat in his class during junior year.

Early in the year, we read Malcolm Gladwell's book *Outliers*. According to Gladwell, it takes ten thousand hours of intensive practice to achieve mastery of complex skills. As you can imagine, I was sitting quietly in the back of the room while everything inside me begged to chime in. Well, Mr. Maguire was so in tune with his students, he called me to the front of the class and asked me to outline my hockey schedule on the board. We added it all up and sure enough there it was, ten thousand–plus hours. At the time I was completely out of my comfort zone and mortified by the attention, but Mr. Maguire also brought validation, focus, and attention to the things I was doing outside of school and drew a correlation between the things I was doing in my athletic life and my personal successes. He showed me that there were people in school who noticed what I was doing outside of class, and that motivated me to be a better student in school.

He still uses me as an example to this day.

Things began to take shape and to make more sense. I began to remember the Kendall who liked her assignment books back at Palos West and who loved completing her homework and checking off the assignments as much as she loved going to her Learn to Play Hockey classes with Coach Bob. Meanwhile, that junior year I was still practicing with the Chicago Mission boys' team and in my second year with the Chicago Mission U19 girls' team. I was just as focused on being the best athlete I could be, and I had as much love for hockey as I ever had in the past. Only now, the sport wasn't consuming every single part of me.

It's not like I fell on my face after hernia surgery and woke up a completely different person. Although I did fall on my face . . . It's more like my time being horizontal made me understand myself a little better, and that I am, in fact, not just a hockey player. I am a human being who happens to play hockey and who has a variety of interests. And it gave me the time to consider what mine might be.

Tapping into my academic and intellectual sides brought me stability. I needed time to let my body rest, to reflect on my accomplishments and failures.

I understood that I would be able to accomplish much more as an athlete if I was a more well-rounded person. Maybe I wouldn't be the most popular kid in school, but oftentimes the path less traveled is the one that leads you to your greatest successes. Get outside your comfort zone, because that's where learning happens. That's part of figuring out your balance.

GOLDEN COYNE

Know your "why." When you know why you're doing something, you're able to motivate yourself when things get tough, and nothing can throw you from your path.

This balance all paid off when I made my second U18 Women's National Team during my junior year. The tournament was held in Fussen, Germany. It would be my first time traveling overseas. Twenty-two women made the team, and I was given the number 19 that year. While I don't know why my number changed, it doesn't matter. As Herb Brooks once said, "The name on the front is a lot more important than the name on the back."

We went on to beat Russia, Germany, and Sweden in the preliminary round. We beat the Czech Republic in the semifinal game, setting up the gold medal game against Canada. The game was tied 2–2 at the end of regulation, and with 6:47 into overtime I scored the game-winning goal. I jumped as high as I could in the air, and before I knew it I was smashed at the bottom of a dog pile, celebrating our second-consecutive gold medal.

Unfortunately, my parents were not there to witness the moment and even worse, there was no coverage of the tournament, so my parents sat at home, in the middle of the day, refreshing the box score on the IIHF website.

When I returned home to Sandburg, the picture of me jumping in the air was on the front page of the local newspaper. When I walked into Mr. Maguire's class, he had a copy of the newspaper plastered on his door.

A year of balance allowed me to accomplish goals on and off the ice and set me up for what was to come next in the college recruiting process.

CHAPTER 17

ALMOST WILL NEVER BE GOOD ENOUGH

Everything has to be earned,
even your failures.

In August of 2009, I was the youngest of forty-one players invited to try out for the Women's National Team that would go on and train together in preparation for the 2010 Winter Olympic Games in Vancouver. To me, this felt like fate. It was everything I had been working toward since the inception of the dream back at Cammi's camp when I was seven. I had imagined a gold medal just like hers around my neck, and suddenly I was one step closer. All the hard work and sacrifice felt worth it, as I had the opportunity to showcase my very best against the very best. However, getting invited to the tryout was just the first part of this process, and now I had to earn my spot on the team.

This tryout camp wasn't like the others. At this point, I had some experience with fierce competition. Ever since I put on a Team USA jersey for the first time in August 2007, I knew I would have to work every single day to make sure I got to keep it on. Being a part of a camp and team at this level is earned, not given or guaranteed, whether it's your first time or your tenth.

I was used to earning my place and fighting to keep it. I knew it was an honor to be where I was, and I couldn't take anything for granted. But at the tryouts in Blaine, Minnesota, the air was thick with tension. It felt intimidating. Unlike in the past, where I sensed I wanted it more and was willing to work harder and sacrifice a little bit more to gain an edge, here *everyone* wanted it as much as me. For some of the postgraduate players, if they didn't make this team, it could mean the end of their hockey careers. There wasn't a professional women's hockey league where they could go to make a living. The National Team was the pinnacle of the sport.

I was lucky. If I didn't make it, I would go back to Sandburg for my senior year of high school, play for the Chicago Mission, and had many years of hockey ahead. If I did make it, people in school would *finally* understand the level of hockey I played. I knew practically no one but Mackenzie would notice my absence for an entire year, but I also knew if I was on the team when the 2010 Winter Olympic Games in Vancouver rolled around, my classmates would see why I'd made the sacrifices and choices I had throughout high school.

To add to the pressure of the moment, I noticed everyone had team-issued navy-blue hockey pants. Since I was a U18 player, I had only gotten the most uncomfortable, saggy, long pant shell that went over my black Chicago Mission hockey pants. When I saw that I was the only one without team pants, I asked the equipment manager if I could have a pair. I wanted to fit in.

He didn't hesitate for a second. "No, you have to earn these, and you haven't earned anything yet."

I turned bright red as I tried to hide my embarrassment. I had no idea those pants needed to be earned! I was off to a hot start. Plain and simple, everything there was for ultra-competitive people like myself, but this was a whole new level, and one that I quickly had to learn to navigate.

GOLDEN COYNE

Always hold yourself accountable to become the best you can be, no matter what obstacle is thrown your way. It is not what you do, but how you do it.

Since I was young and new to the Olympic tryout process, I was looking forward to working with the coaches that week. I always ask coaches a ton of questions. At a normal camp, coaches are constantly giving feedback and letting players know how they can improve. Conversations, meetings, and active discussions are happening all the time. Players live for that. To make it to the elite level, you have to be coachable, able to process feedback and reflect on your performances.

Here, there was silence. Cold, hard stares. Constant, brutally honest assessment.

During Olympic tryouts, the rink is closed to the public. There are locks on the doors and tarps on the windows. The bleachers become tables that are set up for the coaches-turned-evaluators to sit with their pens and notebooks. They watch each player closely, taking notes. It's a tall order not to pay attention to them, not to be thrown off by their facial expressions or a pen squiggling on the paper in front of them when something happens, wondering if the mistake has been noticed. Of course it's been noticed. Nothing slips the coaches' attention.

Add to that the on- and off-ice fitness testing that are musts immediately upon arrival. On the ice we did six three-hundred-yard shuttles, pro-agility, and a sprint test goal line to near blue line. Off the ice we did bench press, vertical jump, pull-ups, sprints, and had our body fat tested. Every single aspect of our physical and mental capacity was under the microscope. The tryout, in a nutshell, comes down to fitness testing, three games in four days, and then it is over. A dream is either earned or not. It's frightening, thrilling, just about every emotion you can imagine. And all the while, everyone is trying to act normal.

Meanwhile, we had to stay in these dreadful dorms that were already impossible to get a good night's rest in. The pillow and mattress were like flotation devices you'd bring on a camping trip, and any time you rolled over, your roommate was put on notice because of the cheap material. Also, there was a communal bathroom that all forty-one of us had to share, so after a mentally and physically exhausting day at the rink, coming back to the dorm wasn't the most decompressing environment either.

At the end of the week, they put all the players in a room. Head coach Mark Johnson read the names of those who had made the team aloud in alphabetical order. Those whose names were not read would be handed a plane ticket by the general manager, Michele Amidon, on the way out the door and would be heading home. Those whose names were read would go on to represent the 2009–2010 Women's National Team and compete for a final spot on the 2010 Olympic Team.

I did my best to meet the moment of truth with grace and dignity. Players of great skill and merit sat around me trying to do the same, but we were balls of nerves, as we had been all week. As names were called and other names were skipped, tears began falling around me. Being near the beginning of the alphabet, I realized pretty quickly when I heard Meghan Duggan's name that they passed right over mine. I was upset, but I kept my tears from escaping my lids and held strong, trying to be happy for those who had triumphed.

Now that I knew my fate, I wanted to be out of that horrible dorm room and on my way home, where my senior year of high school awaited. I wanted to take the time I needed to process everything while I was surrounded by those who knew me best. I wanted to learn from the moment, reflect on the experience, and make sure it didn't happen again.

So when I was handed a plane ticket to Calgary, Alberta, I looked at Michele Amidon and said, "I'm sorry, I think you gave me the wrong one. This says Calgary—I am going home to Chicago." I was sure they had somehow confused two cities that started with *C*.

She looked at me with zero change in her expression. "No, that is correct. You have a game tonight against Team Canada." My jaw just about hit the floor as she continued. "Since you are still eligible for the U18 Select team, you are going to play in the three-game series versus Canada, which starts tonight. You won't be going home today."

For some reason, being sent to Calgary shook me more than anything else in that moment. I found a quiet place at the airport away from the other cut players, pulled out my cheap cell phone

I'd turned off for the announcement meeting, and prepared to call home. While I was sad I had to break the news I had been cut, feeling like I let down my parents, I was looking forward to hearing the friendly sounds of my family. That was until I held down the power button for what felt like an eternity, the phone beeped, showed signs of life, failed, and then gasped before becoming nothing but a cold piece of plastic in my hands right as I was about to get on a plane to Canada. It was cold like everything else just then. I was too self-conscious to ask any of the other players if I could borrow a phone because everyone was extremely emotional as well, wanting to speak to their loved ones in private just like I was attempting to do.

Although I could rationalize what had happened and had enough self-awareness to know some of the reasons why I hadn't made the team. In my opinion, I needed to think more quickly, I needed to get stronger, my shot needed to improve, I needed to get faster (yes, I really did), and I needed to use my speed more effectively. My next chance for the Olympic team would be in four years and that felt so far away in that moment.

While I wasn't going home to be with my family, I was going to Calgary to play hockey for Team USA, and I still had so much going for me. I knew in my heart this was the beginning of the road, not the end. I had work to do, but I needed to do what I had always done: pick myself back up and do the next right thing, which in this case was realizing how lucky I was to be able to put a Team USA jersey back on hours after I'd failed to earn the honor of wearing it and to play in three games against Team Canada.

Fresh off the plane, I lined up for the opening face-off of the first game, and before the puck dropped, I remember a Canadian opponent tapped my shin guards and said, "Don't worry, you'll get there one day." A moment of sportsmanship. We won the first game 4–3 and I scored the opening goal, coming off so much emotion from what transpired the last few hours.

When I did arrive back at Sandburg for my senior year of high school, it was with a whole lot of hockey ahead of me and a decision about college that had to be made.

CHAPTER 18

COLLEGE FIASCO

Everything happens for a reason.

*I*n the middle of my senior year, I realized life is too short for some and making the Olympic team wasn't the end all, be all. On December 23, 2010, my friend and teammate Liz Turgeon was in a car accident and passed away.

It was late in the night, and I was in bed when my phone rang. On the other end was my friend and teammate Alyssa, who I'd become good friends with since the peewee tournament in Quebec. She said in one breath, "Did you hear what happened to Liz, I know you are close with her and wanted to see how you are doing?"

I said no, jumped off my top bunk, and ran to my mom before Alyssa could even tell me what was wrong. I told Mom something happened to Liz. Both of us were devastated as Alyssa broke the news.

Three short days later, I had to get on a plane to attend the annual Women's National Team Holiday Training Camp that started the day after Christmas. After four days at camp, I was given permission to depart early to attend Liz's funeral. My mom met me there.

I had the honor of being a pallbearer. During many moments of my life, I think of Liz—how successful she would have been and how much love she infused into the world. I'm thankful for my wonderful relationship with the entire Turgeon family. I think of Liz every single day. I continued to play in Liz's honor. After all, she had the same Olympic dream as me. I miss my friend.

The next step in my journey was to find the right college.

I knew I was a good player, maybe even a great one given my accolades up to that point, but I still wasn't prepared for the volume of letters that landed in my mailbox, which was upward of twenty each week. I read them all and would lick my thumb and smudge their signature to see if it was handwritten or not. That detail mattered to me because it showed the extra mile the coaches were willing to go, and I knew the extra mile was what it took to be successful. In addition to the letters, the coaches were able to call and email me, so I had different forms of communication coming at me from all different channels.

The attention was overwhelming in a way, but I was too driven and too busy to see the letters and phone calls as anything other than what they were: possible opportunities to earn a college scholarship and a chance to craft a future living for myself, because I knew even if I was good enough, I wasn't going to be able to do that playing professional hockey.

By this time, I was already forced to envision a life after hockey. If Kevin or any other of the hundreds of boys I had played hockey with up to this point had been good enough, they could have explored careers in professional hockey. I didn't have that path no matter what I did, no matter how good I got, no matter what level of success I achieved.

For me, the Olympics represented the pinnacle of success, but it wouldn't ensure a future for me and it certainly wouldn't fund a life. Having been raised and trained by my parents the way I had been, I grasped the reality of my situation, and I took the recruitment process very, very seriously. When I was told repeatedly, by every recruiter, that I was the top recruit in the country, I knew this was my ticket and I was not going to squander it.

After much consideration, I narrowed down my choices to Harvard, Cornell, Minnesota, Wisconsin, and Boston University. I knew I wanted to major in communications, so a strong program was essential.

That year, I played for my third and final season with the Chicago Mission U19 team. All around me, players were silently being plucked and committing to colleges around the country. It wasn't something we discussed for a variety of reasons. For one thing, it would make for a strange dynamic among the players. It was already stressful enough with the individual conversations we were having with college coaches and our families away from the rink. The last thing we needed was for those conversations to become chatter between the players *in* the rink.

When the recruiting process heated up, a lot of players started gripping their sticks too tightly and tried to become the player they thought the college coaches wanted to see. They started to worry more about what was going on outside the rink versus inside the rink and stopped focusing on the task at hand. I reminded myself I needed to play my game to be the best version of myself because that was who these coaches would get if I went to one of their schools.

By the time the spring of my senior year rolled around, just about everyone who was going to play DI college hockey had committed . . . except me. I had decided to do it my way. By then I had already applied to Harvard and Cornell and not gotten in, but I still had plenty of offers on the table. I hadn't closed the door on most of them, and I wouldn't until I'd had the chance to think it through *after* the U18 World Championship. Normally, the tournament was held in January, but because of the Olympics that year it had been delayed until early April.

This was my third and final U18 Women's World Championship, and even more exciting, the tournament was being held at the Chicago Mission's rink—my home rink, coincidentally the same rink Cammi held her hockey camp twelve years earlier. This was a dream. The world was coming to my home. I was ready to enjoy every second of this moment and put the college commitment on pause. It was arguably the biggest decision I had to make up until this point in my life and I didn't want to rush.

With the tournament being at home, there were so many of my family and friends who would finally get a chance to see me play for Team USA for the first time, since we were usually traveling around the world.

We ended up playing Team Canada in the gold medal game. We were up 4–3 halfway through the third period when I got the puck and went from one end of the ice to the other and scored a bar-down goal to put us up 5–3, my second goal of the game, which gave us a much more comfortable lead. The goal judge turned on the red light. Everyone in the rink knew it was a goal, and many were amazed by my end-to-end speed and elite finish. We put our arms up, hugged each other, and went for high fives from our bench. The Canadian players went back to their bench in disappointment. The official who was well behind the play finally made her way down the ice, and waived that there had been no goal.

Everyone—I mean everyone—was stunned. It shocked our bench. As much as our head coach, three-time Olympian Katie King, argued, the IIHF did not have a video replay system installed, so the referee's call stood. The score went back to 4–3. A few shifts later, Canada scored to tie the game 4–4. We went into overtime, and we ended up losing 5–4. It was disappointing for so many reasons. That was the end of my U18 career with Team USA. It's a time in my life I'm still proud of. I remain the all-time leading scorer in IIHF U18 Women's World Championships history with thirty-three points. I had twenty-two goals and eleven assists in fifteen games throughout my three tournaments.

The two things that still bother me are that, in my opinion, we should have had video replay, and four officials opposed to the three they provided—two things that are required in the men's tournament. Arguably, we lost a gold medal because of these differences.

I couldn't control what had happened in that game, but I could control my college decision. Since I had told the coaches I would be making my decision after the U18 World Championships, they started calling as soon as the tournament ended.

It was time.

I sat down with my parents and decided I would attend Boston University because it offered the full package: a stellar communications curriculum, a good hockey team, and a full scholarship.

I thought the right thing to do would be to call all the schools that had offered me scholarships one by one and let them know I wouldn't be accepting their generous offers, and voice how grateful I was for their commitment to communicate with me throughout the process. I wanted to make sure each school heard from me personally before they heard my decision from anyone else.

When I made my last call of the day, to Boston University, the coach didn't answer. I left a message. Exhausted by the whole process, I went and flopped onto Bailey's bottom bunk and immediately dozed off. I woke up to the sounds of our patio door slamming. My mom had been outside on the deck, talking on the phone, and she seemed very angry. I didn't think anything of it and went back to sleep, until I couldn't. Mom came upstairs moments later, totally distraught. I was worried something was seriously wrong. She told me she'd been talking with the head coach of Boston University. I was so confused. At first, I thought the coach missed my call and accidentally called my mom's phone instead. But I could tell something was up. She was livid. My stomach was in knots, and as she explained, it began getting worse.

It turned out he did not have the *full* scholarship he promised in all our letters, emails, phone calls, and home visits during the *entire* recruiting process.

I think the coach had been too afraid to call me back, and instead reached out to my mom, hoping for a softer reaction from her.

Not knowing my complete fate, Mom then handed me her cell phone and I called him back. The coach confirmed what he had told my mom and went on to explain how he would still love for me to attend Boston University, but he only had a partial scholarship. I felt sad, confused, and betrayed. I knew my worth and wasn't accepting anything less. I was a full scholarship–caliber player. Tears streamed down my face as I thought we would be celebrating an exhausting process coming to its well-deserved conclusion.

I had just called and closed the door on every school that had been recruiting me and in a matter of minutes I watched it all crumble. Four months from this moment, I was supposed to be stepping onto a campus in Boston, Massachusetts, accomplishing another goal:

GOLDEN COYNE

Always know your worth and fight for what you know you deserve. Never settle for anything less.

playing DI college hockey. It was a total and complete fiasco; however, this was not going to slow me down. In the meantime, we had some serious regrouping to do, because everything I had planned on, all my careful thinking about my future . . . it had all just been pulled right out from under me without any warning and was totally out of my control. What now?

CHAPTER 19

THE PIVOT

*Change is hard. Control what you can
control: your work ethic and your attitude.*

O nce I had processed my disappointment and the sense of
betrayal following the Boston University fiasco, I wasn't
going to drown in a pool of my own tears. I started by making
some very uncomfortable phone calls to inform all the schools
I had just said no to that I was starting the recruitment process
again and was back to square one. The guidance counselor who
had been with me from day one at Sandburg, Mrs. Blaschek, was
willing to write new letters of recommendation for me since the
spring semester of my senior year was coming to an end. She'd
never seen anything like this, and was fairly confused herself, but
helped me through the chaos every step of the way. This wasn't
how anyone had imagined the end of the year playing out, especially me, but nothing about my life had been a straight shot and
I knew I would recover from this latest, unexpected slam.

Initially, as some full-scholarship offers began rolling in again,
I felt pressured to pivot and figure out what to do next, quickly.

Obviously, based on my past behavior, you can tell that's not something I like to do. I excel at making snap decisions on the ice, but a lot of that is because I'm skilled at anticipating the play before it happens. There was no anticipating this. When it comes to making decisions, I need time to process all the facts as well as the pros and cons, and I want to be able to ask questions if I have them so I can make the very best decision. This was too much to process instantly, especially considering everything I had going on with school and hockey.

When everything felt like it was falling apart in my life—the hardest being losing Liz, to the other things that became so minor, from getting cut from the Olympic Team to losing a gold medal in the fashion we did, and the fiasco with Boston University—I leaned on those who knew me best to get through it all. One of my coaches brought up the idea of attending prep school for a postgraduate year—essentially, a fifth year of high school. That's when everything changed and I felt some of the pressure give.

I had missed a lot of school and knew I could be more academically prepared heading into college. I love learning. I also wasn't in any rush,

GOLDEN COYNE

In tough times, lean on those who love you unconditionally.

since I knew the sooner I got through my four years of college hockey, the sooner I'd be looking for a full-time job, and that job wouldn't be playing the sport I loved.

I contacted a few prep schools that were known for their excellent academics and hockey. I wanted somewhere I could improve myself on both fronts and continue to pursue Team USA. I applied on the fly with one question: Can I practice with the boys' team? I was supposed to be going on to play at the next level, and if I was attending a prep school, I had to be confident that my training environment met my personal standards, which meant skating with the boys' team like I always had. I couldn't afford to be marooned at a school that couldn't give me confirmation I would continue to grow as a player. School after school said no. Only the Berkshire School agreed, so I took a leap of faith and committed to attending the school in the fall, which was literally now twelve weeks away.

Not long before this decision, I had just won my sixth and final state championship and competed in my final USA Hockey National Championship. Shortly after, I'd walked across the stage to collect my diploma from Sandburg. During all these high school years, I'd always thought I would be going on to play Division I college hockey once I graduated, and instead I would be returning to a high school next year. This news also shocked and confused the hockey world. People at the rink would ask me, *Why Berkshire?* Since I didn't have the energy at the time to explain the Boston University fiasco, I'd say I wanted to get an education and an extra year of hockey, which was true and an optimistic way of seeing the situation.

That summer, after also graduating from the U18 Women's National Team, I got invited to be on the U22 National Select Team and play in the U22 three-game series with Team USA in Toronto. This would be my last hurrah before heading off to the Berkshire School. In the second period of the third game of the series, I went into the corner for a puck and got slashed by an opponent. She took her stick and karate chopped it across my wrist to try and slow me down. Players tried to slow me down a

Me as a baby.

Playing catch with Dad outside our rental home in Oak Forest. The rental home was so small and congested, I was always looking to get outside and play.

My first-ever hockey team, the OPIA Jr. Penguins, playing at the United Center for the JuniorHawks game.

A shot from practice during my second year with the Chicago Chill '92s; my jersey number that year was 7, to match Chris Chelios.

Documenting another lost tooth … which was removed with Kevin's help.

A photo from my early basketball days, when I was busy playing every sport I could.

Our famous 1998 family Christmas card with my hero, Cammi Granato: from left to right are Bailey (age 3), me (age 7), Jake (age 5), and Kevin (age 10).

Team Powerade, the first all-girls team to play in the Quebec International Pee-Wee Tournament. I am in the bottom row, second in from the left. Jordan is far left, next to the coaches; Alyssa is fourth in on the top row; and Liz is second from the right in the top row. Manon is in the middle; her son Dylan—in front—was our mascot.

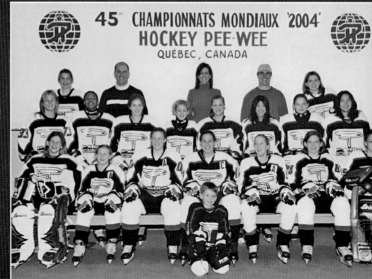

ying for the Oak Lawn Ice. In the right-hand photo, I was playing second ~~se, though I was usually the catcher. Fun fact: the baseball mitt I have on~~ he only mitt I used throughout my softball career. It used to be all black, ~~I~~ was the mitt Dad used in high school.

My fifth-grade school photo with my hair in a braid, holes in the knees of my jeans from shinny, and my favorite shoes (because they didn't have laces to trip on), and of course the shirt that speaks to my love for the game of hockey.

I wore #77 at Northeastern in memory of Liz.

USA Hockey

My parents and me after I accepted the 2016 Patty Kazmaier Award as the best player in Women's DI college hockey.

The first picture Michael and I ever took together, when we first met at our local gym in 2014 ...

... And our wedding photo on July 7, 2018.

Our family now: Me, Michael, and our dog, Blue.

Above: My whole world after becoming an Olympic Champion. From left to right: Jake, me, Michael, Mom, Bailey, Dad, and Kevin.

Right: Right after we won Olympic gold in 2018, Michael was the first one on the ice, and the rest of our family and friends followed his charge.

Celebrating on the field after Michael won Super Bowl 50 with the Denver Broncos on February 7, 2016.

Attendees of the Kendall Coyne Hockey Camp I created in 2016, at the rink where it all started for me, the Arctic Ice Arena (formerly Orland Park Ice Arena).

Chicago Blackhawks

On the ice coaching the Golden Coynes as part of my role as the Chicago Blackhawks' first female player development coach and youth hockey growth specialist.

With Bonnie Vonder Haar, the first time we met.

My first "pitch" at a White Sox game in 2018.

Waiting for the puck to drop while working as an analyst for Notre Dame men's hockey with NBC Sports.

Michael and me supporting our hometown Chicago Red Stars, the National Women's Soccer League team we joined as part of the ownership group.

The 2019 NHL All-Star Fastest Skater Competition. I finished 7th out of eight skaters, with a time of 14.346 seconds, beating Clayton Keller of the Arizona Coyotes.

Billie Jean King and Ilana Kloss dropping the puck at a PWHPA Dream Gap Tour event in Chicago; both Billie Jean and Ilana have been instrumental supporters.

lot, and most times penalties were called and that was the end of it. But this time I knew right away something was wrong. I had played through my hernia saga and had been hurt plenty of times before, but this pain was different. I felt my bone come apart and broke into an icy sweat. I thought I was going to pass out.

I finished the game even though I couldn't catch a pass or shoot a puck. I went to our team doctor, who decided since we were leaving the country the following morning, she would splint me up and get me on a plane, and I would be sent for medical care once we were back in the United States.

My wrist was hanging by a thread. It was not good. The only brace material we had anywhere nearby was an ACE elastic bandage. It was the property of our athletic trainer's college, however, and she refused to give it to us. So the team doctor grabbed a Tupperware container that had been filled with Band-Aids, cut out the bottom of it, then used this bottom piece of the container to create a splint to fit from the palm of my hand to halfway up my arm, and then wrapped it up to hold it in place.

I was in so much pain.

So much pain.

And there was nothing I could do about it.

I had to stay like that for two days, and once I got home, I went to see an orthopedic surgeon who was in-network with our insurance policy. I was placed in a cast. After my pain persisted, I went for a second opinion and that doctor informed me that the first diagnosis was wrong and I had been casted improperly for a week. So I got the proper cast, and for some reason picked a lime-green one that drew attention to me everywhere I went.

As summer neared its end, I got ready to move to Sheffield,

Massachusetts, for the new school year at Berkshire, realizing this whole undertaking was going to be more complicated than I had originally thought. I also knew by then that everything always is. Even with all the ups and downs, including my awful injury and the evermore winding path I seemed to be on, I was so grateful to be where I was. Who knew what was coming next, but whatever it was, my lime-green cast and I were ready.

CHAPTER 20

LIFE UNDER THE MOUNTAIN

*Find ways to challenge
yourself every day.*

The Berkshire School, which was located under a mountain in Massachusetts, was a wonder for me. I had come from a public school of four thousand kids, and I'd just walked into a place with eight to twelve kids to a class, where fierce debates were had over intellectual concepts. Business dress was required, and everyone came with their laptops ready to take notes seriously as the teachers lectured. I took pottery and photography as electives. The classes were intimate and intense. I adapted to business dress, mountain biking, squash, eating in the dining hall, required study hall, half-day classes on Wednesday and Saturday, and so many other things. It was an opportunity and privilege at a level I'd never experienced.

Everyone at Berkshire was required to play three sports, and I was so excited to play softball in the spring. While I had stopped playing after my sophomore year at Sandburg, I still missed the game. This would be my chance to rekindle my love for softball. As for my plan for a sport in the fall, I didn't have one. I had never played any of the traditional fall sports, other than basketball when I was young, because fall was when hockey started back home. I looked on the website and found strength and conditioning as an option, and decided that fit best to achieve my goal of getting stronger for hockey.

Before moving to Sheffield, I made a friend who would turn out to be my first boyfriend. He was a hockey player too. I was eager to get to know him—because at that point, I didn't know anything about the school other than the fact I would have the opportunity to practice with the boys' team. I was also nervous about having to meet a ton of new people at once. As an upperclassman, he was the perfect person to answer a lot of my newbie questions. He seemed really nice, although he did scoff at me when I told him I'd be joining his hockey practices.

"Girls don't practice with the boys' prep team," he said.

"Then I will be the first," I told him.

Other than a few texting conversations I'd had with the future first boyfriend before arriving at school, I knew no one, so my first true friend on campus was assigned: my roommate, Kelsey. Kelsey was wonderful and we became friends right away. We had the same goals of playing Division I sports. Maybe we bonded so quickly because I asked her to please help me put on my clothes, do my hair, and tie my shoes on the first day of school since I couldn't do so with my lime-green cast. That first day is also when I dropped the habit of wearing a braid off the ice. With my injury and living without my mom for the first time, I had to let it go. It may not seem like much, but for so long that was my signature. I had always been the girl with the braid and now I was just . . . me.

I quickly realized I wasn't the only one making concessions because I was away from home. There, under the mountain, the majority of students didn't have their families or their familiar comforts, and in some ways that was a great equalizer.

Since hockey was a winter sport at Berkshire, I understood when I arrived the ice wouldn't be in until November. There was no way I was going to let my skills diminish during the fall season, but at the same time I didn't know the area, didn't know the rinks, didn't have a car, and knew hardly anyone. I had just come off a really good three-game series with U22 Women's Select Team (other than breaking my wrist), so I knew the chance of making my first Women's National Team roster for the Four Nations Cup in November was high. I couldn't stop skating for two whole months and just show up to play in my first-ever Women's National Team international competition. I wanted to know what the hockey kids did. Was there somewhere in town to get ice? Where did they work out? Where did they hang out? What was the culture like? My first boyfriend was the perfect person to answer all my questions.

You know how I said before, everything happens for a reason? Since I was injured before I got to Berkshire, sporting my lovely, obnoxious lime-green cast, I couldn't do strength and conditioning as I had planned. I was put in a group with students who were also injured, and we had low-key physical therapy sessions instead. This was good for my wrist but bad for my personal morale. I was so used to being on a team that I was a little lost without that dimension in my life.

Kelsey saw the impact it had on me. I didn't get to meet many people after school through fall sports like she did, so being the good friend she was, she convinced her coach to let me join the varsity soccer team for a couple of games. She also had to convince *me*. Kelsey promised she would break down everything I needed to know during nightly study hall sessions in our room, so I agreed. When it came time for the game, I was a defender and she was a goaltender, so I wouldn't be too far away from her position in the net.

While she may have been able to give me tips and advice from a distance, she could not put more air in my lungs and keep my legs from feeling like Jell-O. In hockey, we average forty-five-second shifts on the ice and then get a break. In soccer, there are no line changes. I was on the field for the entire eighty-minute game, and I was *so* tired. Still, I am very glad Kelsey pushed me out of my comfort zone. I played a new sport, made new friends, and had a great time. She was a great roommate, teammate, and friend. She went on to play DI soccer.

And overall, while there were kids at the school who came from wealth, you would never know it. They didn't flaunt it or judge others for not having it. The Berkshire culture was so diverse and welcoming that people really got to know each other before making preconceived judgments about their classmates, which I loved and learned to emulate.

A little over a month into Berkshire, I was starting to fully understand what it felt like to live away from home. It was exhausting for so many reasons! It was finally time for my lime-green cast to come off, and my mom wasn't there to help. So the athletic trainer took me to a doctor in town to get the cast off, and I was given a removable cast with two metal bars—one on the top and one on the bottom that wrapped around the palm of my hand. My directions were to wear the cast whenever I wanted. I was ready to get back to work in the weight room doing the things I hadn't been able to do with a cast, including Olympic lifts such as cleans—pulling a barbell with added weight off the floor to then catch it in a squatting position with the bar on your shoulders. One day I was doing just that, and when I performed the catch, I heard a raging pop in my wrist. I knew it was bad. *Shoot*, I thought. At that point, I wasn't sure what to do other than wear the removable soft cast to mitigate the pain until I could go back home and see the doctor.

A couple of days later, I was invited to attend the espnW summit across the country in La Jolla, California. The espnW brand launched at that summit, which was thrilling on multiple levels. Not only did I get to meet the legendary Billie Jean King, I was excited to be on the "Voices of the Future" panel with star basketball player Skylar Diggins-Smith and phenomenal snowboarder Maddy Schaffrick. It was a huge honor and yet another new door opening for me. *Someone wanted to listen to me talk?* I could feel this momentum building, and I knew if I stayed the course, I really could be a voice for the future. The feeling of hopelessness I'd had less than a year before had been replaced with anticipation for what was to come.

When I got back from the summit, I then got an invitation from the Women's National Team general manager for the Four Nations Cup in St. John's, Newfoundland. This would be my first international competition with *the* Women's National Team. My wrist was still busted, but I wasn't going to let that stop me. I scored my first Women's National Team goal against Team Canada in the gold medal game. I still have the puck to this day.

Once we started hockey at Berkshire, I had no time to waste. At first, the boys' team was confused about why I was skating with them, but I didn't care. I was there to be pushed, to prepare, and to work. The coach explained exactly that to the team, and that I was on Team USA, and added they should admire my determination to be prepared.

In the twenty-five games I played at Berkshire, I had fifty-five goals and twenty-two assists, which added up to seventy-seven points. I've never cared about points—I care about wins. But seventy-seven was important to me. That was Liz's number.

On a scheduled winter break in February, I went back home to Chicago to be with my family to make a final college decision once again. It was important to me to be with my parents because their hard work and sacrifices had gotten me where I was. On Super Bowl Sunday in 2011, I decided that in six months from that day, I'd be stepping onto a college campus in Boston, Massachusetts . . .

This time at Northeastern University as a Husky.

I had formed a relationship with the head coach, Dave Flint, who was willing to be as hands-off or hands-on as I wanted throughout my process. He cared about me as a person and not just as a player. Northeastern also had a great communications school and a co-op program that could offer me work experience while getting school credit. I already knew at some point I wanted to work in sports and dreamed of someday working for the Blackhawks, so that met my needs. Northeastern also had a calm, quiet, diverse energy to it. I didn't want parties and noise and madness. I needed somewhere I could focus.

I wasn't too concerned about the school's hockey ranking, which was not the best. The team had never been to the NCAA tournament, and I was determined to help get it there. Only the top eight teams earned a berth in the tournament, and just like the Olympics, it was another goal I felt determined to accomplish and would not be satisfied otherwise. While it wouldn't be easy at all, I believed in my resiliency when it came to facing new challenges. I couldn't wait to meet that challenge head-on.

This second time around, I again called the other schools that had been interested in me and told them I wouldn't be attending, and thanked them very much for their time and effort—especially those who gave me a second chance. I called Coach Flint and he didn't pick up. I panicked, thinking it was happening again. After everything I'd been through, he was going to tell me there was no scholarship and that I was going to have to find another way to make my dream come true. It was already late at night by then, and I had to go back to Berkshire early in the morning, so I went to bed with no communication from Coach Flint.

GOLDEN COYNE

Sometimes the biggest challenges yield the most satisfying results.

I didn't sleep much. Mom drove me to Midway Airport in the morning to head back to Berkshire. About ten minutes from the airport, my phone rang. It was Coach Flint calling me back. I told him my decision, and we had an exciting conversation. I was one the biggest recruits he'd ever landed. My commitment helped change the complexion of the school's hockey program, and my own life whether I knew it or not. The arduous process had finally ended.

And after securing my college future, that spring I played in my first IIHF Women's World Championship with the National Team in Zurich, Switzerland. I was the youngest player on the team and was given the number 26. It was the first time I'd received this number. *Cool*, I thought; little did I know it would become mine. Most importantly, I helped our team win gold. In five games, I scored four goals, which tied for second on the team, had two assists, and a plus-nine rating. That meant I was on the ice for nine goals for my team. (Power play goals do not count toward your plus/minus, and if I was on the ice for any goals against, that would be considered a minus.)

Immediately afterward, I was able to get on a plane from Zurich and head to Chicago to have surgery to repair my damaged wrist. To cap everything off, after surgery, I flew back to Berkshire, this time with a blue cast, and graduated high school for the second time.

For me, all the ups and downs of the last year finally felt like they were smoothing out and, at last, were finding their place. I was on my way toward the next part of my hockey career, which would change me and my life in ways I couldn't have imagined.

CHAPTER 21

BECOMING A HUSKY

*You will learn more from your
failures than your successes.*

I flew into Boston excited for this new chapter of my life, and ready to work hard to meet my educational goals, meet my teammates, and get cracking on the work it would take to bring some championships to Northeastern. Being a student athlete has some advantages, like the sense of immediate inclusion. Walking on campus and being a part of a team, surrounded by people who share your interests in a sport you are there to play, is a comforting feeling. I had a home away from home. Even though Northeastern women's hockey did not have a lot of recent success, there was a buzz around the nine incoming freshmen.

At the same time I was reveling in the buzz around the women's hockey team, I had school to contend with. I sat down with my athletic academic advisor, who was taken aback by the certainty of my academic ambition. I had a five-year scholarship, and I wanted to get a master's in that time. I also wanted a plan fully laid out in advance, so I knew how we'd get it accomplished. That plan would mean taking extra classes most semesters. A total of twenty hours each semester, which is a heavy load. Many student athletes start off by taking the easiest classes possible when they enter college, so they can get acclimated to the demands of juggling academics and sport. When my advisor tried to suggest that those easier classes would be a good fit for me, I told her I had no interest in the commonly traveled path. I was there to learn and to get as much out of my education as possible. She had to adjust her approach in working with me, but by the time the meeting was over, she understood what I planned to do. I wanted my bachelor's degree in Communication Studies, a minor in Business, and a master's in Corporate and Organizational Communication by the time my scholarship ran out . . . and whatever I had to do to make that happen, that's what I was going to do.

GOLDEN COYNE

So often, we want to follow the beaten path, and want to fit in because it is comfortable to be like everyone else, but if you are trying to accomplish something very few have, you will need to do what most aren't willing to do.

Ann Doherty, who I played with on the Team Illinois U14 team, had stayed friends, so when I found out she was going to Northeastern, I requested her as a roommate. There were other freshmen in nearby dorms who were nice and in the same situation as us, trying to get acclimated and find people to hang out with.

There was one other thing I requested. It was my number. "It will be seventy-seven," I said to Coach Flint, "in honor of Liz." Her last hockey number before she passed was 87, but when Liz and I first played together at eleven years old, she was number 77, and that number will always be hers to me. It was now my honor to wear it.

One of the very first tasks we had as a team was off-ice fitness testing. Thankfully, I had plenty of experience with this from the Women's National Team. However, I didn't expect my numbers to be far greater than my teammates especially as a freshman. That's when I realized that as a whole, we needed to pay more attention to the work it took to be strong off the ice in order to lead to success on the ice. I knew I was lucky to learn this valuable lesson at such a young age, when Chuey prevented the forty-five-pound plate from crushing my head because I wasn't strong enough.

Trust me, I get it. There is so much more to college than hockey! I promise, I really do get that. But when we were at hockey and working out for those few hours, we needed to be *all in*, present in the moment, and focused on the task at hand. As soon as we left the rink, minds could go elsewhere.

I decided to lead by example and do what I'd always done: control my work ethic and my attitude, settle for nothing less than my very best, and hope the others would follow suit. At the same time, I still wanted to make an Olympic team. If I was going to accomplish that, I couldn't let my skills or my mindset slide.

Our freshman class of nine players was large and threatening to the upperclassmen, which was part of Coach Flint's initiative to improve Northeastern's team on and off the ice. We were new blood and we brought in new energy and focus.

I did my best to adjust, but during our first few weeks of practice together, a teammate—not an opponent this time—slashed my wrist so hard that it broke. Fresh off a summer surgery, it was busted again. It wasn't tied to a fierce battle in the corner. To me, it was because a teammate was envious of my abilities and playing time.

After practice, I had to go to the hospital to get an X-ray and a new colored cast, which happened to be on the same night as the rookie party. While the cast meant I had to start the healing process all over, being at the hospital meant I couldn't attend the rookie party. Some of my teammates had been giving me a hard time in the first few weeks on campus because I'd told them I didn't drink alcohol. I expected some people to put pressure on me to drink at the rookie party. I was fully prepared to tell them no and ask them to respect my choices. While I didn't think it was a responsible or positive choice to drink while underage, and I had no intention of drinking when I became of age, I knew I could have just as much fun as everyone else without alcohol. But I also understood that my choices were personal. Still, I was sick of negotiating other people's opinions about my choices. A lesson to be learned here is to embrace others' differences and personal choices by understanding their why and don't give in to peer pressure.

When you're part of a team, every decision you make—good or bad—has an effect on everyone else and can become a reflection of the team. You have to take responsibility for your own behavior and decisions, and you also have to be very careful who you allow into your space. As hard as it may be to not give in to peer pressure and follow everyone else's lead, it is important to lead yourself and your life in the direction that you feel is right in your heart.

Thankfully, in spite of some of those early difficulties, we started having success on the ice. The accountability the nine freshmen brought in was tremendous. The upperclassmen didn't want to start losing ice time to freshmen and saw how hard we were working, so they upped their game. And when it came time to win a championship, we were prepared.

Since 1979, on the first and second Tuesdays of February, the annual Beanpot Tournament is played between Northeastern University, Harvard University, Boston College, and Boston University, which are all rival schools. The host site of the tournament is rotated among the four schools, while the men have a permanent home at TD Garden, home of the Boston Bruins (and I firmly believe and have advocated that the women should be playing there too). At first, it seemed like a small tournament to me since it was only between four schools, which meant you started off in a semifinal game, but soon enough I understood the tournament's rich history in Boston. You must know history to make history . . . It was a holiday to the locals, and for the New England natives on my team this was something they had attended as kids and dreamed about winning their whole lives. We did just that.

We won the Beanpot for the first time in fourteen years, bringing a championship back to Huntington Avenue. You better believe beating Boston University—at their home rink—in the Beanpot final held extra-special significance for me during my first year as a Husky. I got the game-tying goal and assisted on the game-winning goal in overtime. Mom even caught a flight to Boston, and Kevin—who was a junior at Becker College only forty-five minutes from Boston—attended the occasion as well.

That was just the beginning of Northeastern making its

move toward being a contender. We started winning regularly. That year we were the Hockey East regular season champions, the first time in program history, and senior goaltender and four-time Swiss Olympian Florence Schelling had a lot to do with it. We worked hard, we maintained a strong mindset and drive, and things started to shift and change.

That April as my freshman year ended, I went on to play in my second IIHF Women's World Championship in Burlington, Vermont, where we lost to Canada 5–4 in overtime despite a huge effort in front of a sold-out home crowd. I was named the US Player of the Game in the final.

All in all, freshman year was a whirlwind, as it started with the Women's National Team August Festival followed by my start at Northeastern, then leaving to play for the Four Nations Cup in November, traveling to the Women's National Team Holiday Camp in December, and then the IIHF Women's World Championships in April—all between a thirty-one-game freshman campaign and a rigorous course load. I was ready to head home to Palos Heights.

My wrist pain had persisted from the first time I broke it in 2010, and the surgery after my first World Championship and the break at the start of freshman season hadn't helped, so in the summer of 2012 I was fed up. Playing hockey had become a miserable experience. It hurt to catch a pass, shoot a puck, stickhandle, work out, do really anything because my wrist was in such bad shape.

It was time to get it properly fixed. After X-rays and an MRI, Dr. Thomas Wiedrich, the best in the world, diagnosed my injury and developed a plan. As part of that plan, I requested he put fifty goals in my wrist—he said no problem! The good news was I had full confidence in him. The bad news: my wrist was really messed up and I would need two surgeries, including one that would require screws and a plate and a six- to eight-month recovery, which I didn't have at the time. I refused to miss the start of my sophomore year at Northeastern, and the following year I had the Olympic tryouts I had been eying since I got cut from the 2010 team. Thankfully, he helped me manage my pain throughout with strategically planned cortisone injections.

Once we decided I'd get my first major operation right after the 2014 Olympics (if I made the team, that is), I turned my attention back to the team at Northeastern and my summer training. It had been such a challenging season, and after reflecting on it back home, I called Coach Flint when I got home and told him a lot needed to change, and I explained what my gut was telling me. Team culture was number one on my mind. I think he was a little shocked that I was having this conversation with him as a rising sophomore, but I knew it needed to happen if change was going to be made.

Sophomore year, Ann and I moved back to campus along with two other teammates as roommates. One was Chelseia Goll, who'd grown up in Boston and had the most wonderful accent to show for it. Jokingly, she would always say I had the strongest "Chicago" accent ever, which I didn't realize until she pointed it out, but she may have been right! Ann and I had grown up playing against Chelseia and really got along well with her freshman year. Our fourth roommate was a player from Canada. Being a sophomore comes with a little more confidence. You've made some friends on campus outside of hockey, you know your way around, and you're not the youngest anymore. I was starting to find my niche.

I met with the Northeastern Athletic Department's production team and asked if I could get broadcasting experience, and before I knew it, I'd secured a spot to work as a sideline reporter for the men's hockey team whenever my schedule allowed. I started finding ways I could enhance my on-campus experience outside of hockey because I knew when the time came, I wanted to do my co-op with the Chicago Blackhawks, and getting as much experience as I could would only help my chances.

Inside the rink, we had another good season with a few slight shifts in our culture. We won the Beanpot for the second year in a row, which made us "Best in Boston" once again. We played Boston University in the opening game and we beat them 4–1, which again was a great feeling. We also *almost* made it into the NCAA tournament, but almost is never good enough.

Eight teams make it into the NCAAs, and we were slivers away from being that eighth team. (It's a mystery how that calculation is made, but that's another conversation.) In two short years, we went from being unranked to almost eighth and making the NCAAs. We had it in us, and we had to use this defeat as motivation to make the NCAA tournament.

I was so mad when we didn't make it. I know I am incredibly driven, but this was a moment everyone needed to be too. We *all* needed to be mad that we didn't make it and use it as fuel. We were so close to making program history and we came up short. One thing I'd learned from the Women's National Team mental skills coach, Dr. Colleen Hacker, was the aggregation of marginal gains. As a team, if we all worked every single day to be one percent better, those small gains in each player would add up to magnificent ones. After we didn't make it to the NCAAs, I tried to get that across to my team.

I was comparatively lucky. Just as everyone was ready to pack away their hockey equipment for the season, I still had more hockey to play. Really important hockey. I was headed to my third IIHF Women's World Championship in Ottawa, Ontario. We beat Canada 3–2 in front of their home crowd of 13,776 at Scotiabank Place, home of the Ottawa Senators. While it was challenging missing two weeks of school each semester my first two years in college for the Four Nations Cup and the IIHF Women's World Championships, I worked with my professors so I could complete my schoolwork while on the road. Nothing was going to stop me from being at these tournaments, because I knew it was the path that would lead me to my first shot at being named to an Olympic team.

CHAPTER 22

DREAM VERSUS REALITY

"All of our dreams can come true, if we have the courage to pursue them."

WALT DISNEY

Forty-one players were invited to Lake Placid, New York, to try out for the 2013–2014 Women's National Team in hopes of earning a spot on the 2014 Olympic roster. The process was no different from the one I'd gone through in 2009: a week long, with on- and off-ice fitness testing and three inter-squad games in four days. I was no longer the inexperienced player I was in 2009. I had already played in three IIHF Women's World Championships, three U18 IIHF Women's World Championships, and four Four Nations Cups. My consistent presence on the Women's National Team gave me the experience I needed to be confident.

At the end of the tryout, we all sat in a room when the head coach, Katey Stone, pulled out her list with the final names. This time mine was called and I was one of twenty-five players named to the 2013–2014 Women's National Team, a roster that would have to get down to twenty-one before the 2014 Olympic Games.

I notified Coach Flint that I had made it and would be taking the year off. He wasn't taken by surprise. When I was going through the recruiting process, every school knew there was a possibility of this happening, especially because college-age players who are named to the National Team Roster in an Olympic year are expected to take the year off from school to focus on training for Team USA. That fall I reported to Bedford, Massachusetts, a town close to Boston where USA Hockey had decided we'd make our home for the year.

For the first time ever in my life, everything was about hockey. I know what you're thinking; nothing new—but this was actually the real thing. *All hockey!* There was no school to think about, no homework, no classes, nothing. Once again, I was experiencing a new level of intensity to go along with this process. Practices were more focused than ever, training was demanding, and my time was never my own.

Mike Boyle was our strength and conditioning coach. Each morning, Mike spent a couple of hours training us at his gym in Woburn. He developed thorough plans to ensure we were in the best shape off the ice but more importantly remained healthy. Afterward, we would get in our cars and head to the rink for a solid two hours on the ice. Coach Stone was tough and demanded excellence from us—which is to be expected in order to make an Olympic team.

Since we had twenty-five players and only twenty-one were going to the Olympics, we were constantly walking on eggshells because everything we did was under a microscope. As much as it was thrilling to be a huge step closer to being named to my first Olympic team, I never felt I could let down my guard, and I was right. Cuts were being made as the residency went on, and the roster wouldn't be finalized until the new year. It was a brutal and seemingly random process because we never knew when someone would go. It's like the worst, most heartbreaking reality show ever.

Players were given a modest stipend, which was not nearly enough to rent a place to live outside of Boston, eat, and pay for other living expenses. There was no time to get a second job to pay for all those things either, so I was graciously taken in by an amazing billet family, the Beveridges, which included eight-year-old Gusty, six-year-old Callen, and their parents Jen and John. The whole family was entrenched in sports, so they understood what I was contending with and were supportive, creating a warm, soft place to return to after a long day of training. To this day, I am so thankful to the Beveridges for opening their home and welcoming me to their family.

And having extra support was a good thing because our coaching staff was not messing around. When we played in the Four Nations Cup in Lake Placid, Dad flew in for it along with many of the players' families and loved ones. There weren't many opportunities for our families to see us over the course of the year, let alone see us play, so this was a splurge and we hoped to spend time together. Our team got the bronze, which was the worst finish ever for the United States, and Coach Stone was not happy. Neither were we.

She came into the locker room after the game and announced we would have only a few minutes to spend with our guests, who we hadn't been able to see throughout the tournament because they were considered a distraction. We had been working so hard, giving it everything we had, and then we could barely even greet the people who had come so far to see us. She was unmoved and claimed any more time than that would be a disturbance for the team.

I'd had Coach Stone's voice in my head since I was fifteen, when she was my first-ever U18 coach and was demanding excellence then. Over the years, she pushed me harder and further than I knew I could be pushed. But this third-place finish made me realize we needed more joy in the process. We needed some love, some of that balance I talked about before.

It all came to a head for me hours after our loss. When our bus got back to Bedford from Lake Placid at four a.m., I, along with six other players, was told to stay back to be disciplined by the goalie coach, Robb Stauber. According to him, I wasn't properly tracking the puck and that was the reason I couldn't score a goal if I received a backdoor pass. But that wasn't the reason we got bronze at the Four Nations Cup.

I have a lazy eye.

I always have.

It's especially lazy when I'm tired, and I was tired all the time then. So while my lazy eye was more obvious, I was confident it wasn't hindering my abilities on the ice, as I had it checked every year by my ophthalmologist, and he never found my eye to be restricting. Robb told us the optometrist he'd used when he played would be flying in from Minnesota to do vision training with us for twenty hours a week after practice to strengthen the muscles in our eyes. I wasn't happy about that because I had been under the close care of an ophthalmologist since I was young and knew exactly what was going on with my eyes. This was a moment I needed to stand up for myself, even if it meant I would get cut.

I spoke to Robb and Coach Stone the next day and told them I wanted to consult with my doctor about the eye program. Maybe Robb was right, and my lazy eye had become a problem since my last checkup. On our next off day, I flew in and out of Chicago in less than twenty-four hours to see my eye doctor. He dilated my eyes and ran a few tests to see if my lazy eye was preventing me from tracking the puck like my coaches believed. He concluded I had no issues tracking in either eye and my vision was still perfect, plus after his consult, he felt there was no need for me to do the eye program prescribed by an optometrist he didn't know. My eyes were in great shape, and he didn't want me messing with them. I went back and gave the report to Robb and Coach Stone the next day after practice.

Well, you can guess how well that went.

A couple of days later we were preparing for a Pre-Olympic Tour game against Canada in Burlington, Vermont. Coach Stone asked to speak to me after the pre-game skate. I thought for sure this was the end of the road, journey, and dream for me. She was extra hard on me at the pre-game skate, to the extent my teammates asked if everything was okay. I shook it off even though I was getting more and more nervous about what was to come. When I got off the bus, she and the assistant coach, Hilary Witt—who was also my coach at Northeastern during my first two years—told me they didn't think I had what it took to make the team. According to Coach Stone, I wasn't willing to commit myself to do whatever was asked of me.

As disappointed as I was, I wouldn't budge. I needed to stay true to what I knew was right. I asked her, "Have you come to this conclusion because of what you've seen in me on the ice and in the weight room this year? Or is this because I'm not willing to do Robb's eye program?"

She didn't give me a straight answer, only said she didn't think I was willing to put in the work. I went from disappointed to angry. I couldn't believe the person who had coached me for so many years with Team USA was questioning my work ethic. I felt like she'd suddenly forgotten all she'd learned about me as a player and person during this time. This team had been the focal point of my life since I was fifteen years old. I didn't know what to make of the conversation. What I did know was that I was going to continue to give my very best and prove I belonged on the Olympic Team.

The conversation continued as we sat outside the hotel, and I had a perfect view of beautiful Lake Champlain. I said to her, "If you ask me to run around that lake one hundred times, I will do it a hundred and one; if you ask me to sit on the ice and receive backdoor passes you don't feel I can track, I will do that for twenty hours a week; but when you ask me to do something that my ophthalmologist has advised me not to do, and I only get one set of eyes for the rest of my life, I need to draw the line."

That was the end of the conversation. I was proud of myself but once again scared for what was to come. I was back to being exhausted, sitting in my room before the game, thinking I was getting cut, walking on eggshells.

They made the final two cuts on December 20, 2013, after our last Pre-Olympic Tour game in Grand Forks, North Dakota. I finally knew my place was secure. I would be heading to Sochi, Russia, to play in the 2014 Winter Olympic Games. My childhood dream was finally coming true.

The next day, I was allowed to fly home for Christmas and spend a couple of days with my family, and that's when I broke the news to them. I wanted to wait until we were eating dinner as a family—our favorite thing to do together, especially Mom's.

On January 1, 2014, the team was announced at the Big House in Ann Arbor, Michigan. My phone went bonkers. People I had known forever and people I had just met all congratulated me. I felt like all the sacrifices I made and my hard work for all those years was paying off. The last five months had been tough, but it was all going to be worth it. I posted a picture of myself on Facebook that had been taken during the announcement at the Big House with a quote from Walt Disney underneath: "All of our dreams can come true, if we have the courage to pursue them." It perfectly summed up how I felt.

Then it was all happening. We flew back to New England to pack our bags for the Olympics and had a police escort from the Bedford rink to the Boston airport as we got on our plane for our first stop in Munich, Germany. There we went through Olympic Team Processing. It was so cool. Everyone who's been to the Olympics says not to pack much, and they're right. You get three suitcases filled with stuff. Each player is given their opening and closing ceremony outfits, tailored just to their liking. You also get your podium outfit and a commemorative ring. It's a special feeling that warrants so much honor—receiving these items that mean you are about to represent the United States of America in the Olympic Games. After all, these are outfits you can't buy; they can only be earned.

We then left on a chartered flight to Sochi, Russia, with an outfit ready to go for each day. We were so excited, you could feel the energy on the plane. Unfortunately, we never got to wear the opening ceremonies outfit. We had a game against Finland the next day so we couldn't walk. We wanted to be there so badly, representing our country, but we watched it together on TV in the Olympic Village.

We didn't attend other events or see our families without permission from our coaches. One day we had practice at the same time the US men's team had a game. They were playing Team Russia, and someone asked Coach Stone if we could catch the end of the game. She was hesitant to say yes, but it was enough of a yes and green light for me to sprint over to the rink to catch the end of one of the most epic hockey games I have ever witnessed in my life. T.J. Oshie, aka T.J. Sochi, scored *six* times in the shootout to defeat the Russians on home ice. It was magical.

We played our five games in twelve days. Five months of preparation for five games. A lifetime of dreaming for five games. We opened up against Finland and won 3–1. We then played Switzerland. Before the game, I got pulled into the mix zone by Hall of Fame broadcaster Mike "Doc" Emrick, who asked me questions about my relationship with former Husky teammate, and current Swiss goaltender, Florence Schelling. I thought it was so special that the greatest of all time was calling our games—even though I didn't get to hear the broadcast. We won 9–0, and I scored my first Olympic goal against Florence. It was awkward because the puck went in, Florence took it out and the official didn't see it, and the play went on. My teammate, Amanda Kessel, picked up the puck and scored again in the same shift. Officials went back and looked at my goal and realized it went in, so then they disallowed Amanda's goal and counted mine, which I felt bad about.

The third and final preliminary game was against Team Canada and we lost 3–2. We still earned a spot in the semifinal, where we defeated Sweden 6–1. Three days later, we played Team Canada in the gold medal game. The last gold medal Team USA had won was Cammi's in 1998, so there was a lot of pressure on us to win.

We had a 2–0 lead with three minutes and thirty-six seconds left in the game. All we had to do was possess the puck and shut them down for less than four minutes. Easier said than done, let me tell you. They scored and then scored again with fifty-five seconds left in the game to tie it up. We went into overtime, which was four on four. Until we took a penalty, making it four on three, and with eleven minutes and fifty seconds left in overtime, they used the advantage to score a power play goal and win.

We lost the gold. I was on a line with Brianna "Decks" Decker and Amanda Kessel, who I had been on a line with for years. The three of us were young but dynamite. We had a motor, chemistry, and skillset to our game that was hard to stop. Each of us tied for the team lead in points with six, and together, we were plus-twenty-four. Another thing that was engrained in us by Dr. Hacker was to know your role, do your role, and embrace your role. It couldn't have been truer at the world stage, and no matter what your role was—it was important.

You learn to do whatever task is asked of you. Nonetheless, I was devastated not to win the gold and was plagued by shoulda, woulda, coulda thoughts.

Because the hockey tournament spans the entire duration of the Olympics, the only thing left for us to enjoy was the closing ceremonies, which only added to the punch-in-the-gut feeling, until we found out our fearless leader and four-time Olympian Julie Chu was named Team USA's closing ceremony flag bearer. That was a big deal. I was so happy for Chuey. I knew this was likely the end of her playing career and had wanted the gold medal so badly for her. She was a great leader, teammate, and friend and deserved this honor. While we lost the Olympics, Chuey's reward was a win for all of Team USA.

One of the most truly special moments I had during my time in Sochi was when I finally got to see my whole family. We'd never gone on vacations because they were too expensive, so it made me extra happy that this trip was their first time traveling out of North America. While I was the one competing in the Olympics, I wouldn't have gotten there without their sacrifice and commitment, and to be able to see all of them at the Olympics meant everything to me. However, once again we were given very limited time to spend together and there was so much to catch up on. The whole experience, while being exhilarating, had also taught me so much.

I think about my first Olympics with mixed feelings. It pushed me in ways I didn't know I could be pushed. Making the Olympic team is *hard*. In a lot of ways, the Olympic team experience shaped me into the player I am now, taught me the level of discipline required, and gave me the perspective I needed to walk into Northeastern and be a leader.

When I got home, I was beyond surprised to discover that people didn't care about our defeat. My hometown of Palos Heights had signs all over congratulating me, and Palos West and Palos South had signs out front too. The teachers from Sandberg had T-shirts with my name and number on them. When I did visits in the community, people only cared that I had been a part of Team USA at the Olympics, and the silver medal was just an extra bonus; they jumped up and down and were excited to meet me. It was illuminating to understand that my own perfectionism didn't reflect the general consensus. People were proud of me and our team, and nothing kept me going more than that. I figured out in high school that being a perfectionist can be draining, and getting silver at the Olympics confirmed it. I always want to be the best I can be; that year I realized that sometimes it's what you've experienced throughout the process that is the win. I had learned to stand my ground, experienced tough love on a whole new level, and realized I could be pushed to work harder than I ever had before. I hadn't gotten the medal I wanted, but I had collected so much gold.

GOLDEN COYNE

Even when a dream doesn't go perfectly, learn from the pursuit and be proud of what you've achieved.

CHAPTER 23

FINDING MY VOICE

*Make the most of each day. As
Eleanor Roosevelt said, "Tomorrow
is a mystery. Today is a gift. That is
why it is called the present."*

From the time I first laid my eyes on Cammi's Olympic gold medal at seven years old, everything in my life had been about getting one just like it. Now I had semi-fulfilled that dream by bringing home the silver, and it sent my life into hyperspeed. I knew the importance of visibility because of how much meeting Cammi had affected my life, and now I was starting see and feel the prestige of being an Olympian. For me, it felt like winning that medal came with a responsibility to inspire others and I was determined to show up as much as I could in as many ways as I could.

Meanwhile, Palos Heights being so proud of my accomplishments made me feel better, and that inspired me to want to give back to the community. I understood how much the Olympics meant to them because of how much the Games had always meant to me. They're a symbol of global unity and an ability for the world to come together through sport.

I was also so humbled that through my efforts in sport, I was able to impact people's day or inspire them somehow. If my dream was to go to the Olympics and I accomplished it, others could accomplish their dreams too. After all, my parents didn't play hockey. My dad can't even skate! I felt this new and exciting responsibility to convey that message, so I overcame my fear of public speaking and went to elementary schools, middle schools, and high schools to share my story.

Being out in the world wasn't always easy, though. Sometimes it was emotional and bittersweet. At one point someone reached out to Dad about meeting a young hockey player, Bonnie, who had recently been diagnosed with Acute Myeloid Leukemia (AML). One of our closest family friends had lost their fourteen-year-old daughter, Julianne Doody, to AML in 2002. After her death, the Doody family courageously started the For Julie Foundation dedicated to leukemia research and helping families affected by the disease. After ten years they raised over one million dollars. That one small family has made a huge difference helping countless families and funding groundbreaking research. Every year while I was growing up, the Doody family would hold a Friday for Julie event, where people would come and do a walk around the town. My family would help with the event. At eleven years old, I would move pizzas from one place to another and put signs up on the walking route. Because I had the opportunity to give back and see the impact helping others can have every year at Friday for Julie, I developed a profound passion for doing what I could to make a difference in people's lives.

So when Dad got this request about a young hockey player who was battling the same blood cancer Julianne had, I was eager to meet her. Dad and I went to see her in the hospital, and I saw the joy the visit brought her. It was so overwhelming to realize my presence might matter to someone who is in the process of fighting literally the battle of her life. We showed each other our jerseys, I showed her my medal, she showed me pictures of her playing hockey, and I did the same. It was like we already knew each other because we had so much in common. We even shared a favorite coach, Kenny McCudden, and a favorite number—77. Bonnie had the biggest smile on her face the entire time, and it's one I'll never forget.

After the visit, we had a quiet forty-five-minute drive back home. Neither Dad nor I were in the mood to talk. I couldn't stop thinking of the next time I would get to see Bonnie or if there was anything I could do to help. She and I stayed in touch for months, until one day her mom called to let me know Bonnie had been called to heaven and was no longer fighting. Tears poured down my face. I was one of the lucky ones that got to know Bonnie Vonder Haar in her short twelve years on earth. She had so much life ahead of her and it was taken from her all too soon.

With the Olympics ending in February, I wasn't going back to Northeastern until the fall, so I said yes to as many appearances as I could, everywhere, especially at home. I did every interview, visited every school I could, every library I could, every hospital I could, and did every community event, including hosting an Olympic Day at the Ronald McDonald House in Chicago. Seeing the change, voice, and inspiration my new platform provided me only fueled my desire to be in the community.

Other than sharing my medal, taking pictures, and signing autographs after speaking about my Olympic experience, one of the focal points of my speeches was about my wrist, which people always asked about since I had a cast. See, as soon as I got home from Sochi, I was in the operating room, *finally* getting my wrist fixed according to Dr. Wiedrich's plan. After surgery I was given a white cast that went from my hand to above my elbow, and the best part was being able to pick out the color of the Velcro straps that held my cast in place. Guess what colors I picked: lime green . . just kidding! Red, white, and blue! After speeches, the first question I would get was, "What happened to your arm?" I explained what happened, because adversity is a big part of everyone's journey, and in many ways it's how you respond to it that defines you. My five-year wrist problems were a little glimpse into some of the adversity I had faced throughout my career.

> **GOLDEN COYNE**
>
> *How you respond to adversity is a big part of who you are.*

In addition to everything else I was doing back home, I got my dream co-op and started working with the Chicago Blackhawks Media Relations Department as an intern.

I would go to the rink four hours before games to set up everything we would need for the media. I got stats ready and basically did whatever they wanted me to do. Through that internship I realized it was actually much easier to play the sport than it was to work it behind the scenes. I did love the meals in the press box, though. We got dinner before games, then food between periods, plus snacks all night long. There's a joke that the NHL stands for the "Never Hungry League," and it took me a while to realize this was normal! I loved every second of being close to my favorite team, and as a special bonus, since I arrived four hours before games, I got to see the new generation of JuniorHawks games before the Blackhawks played. There was something so special about watching those young kids play, knowing that was my beginning too, where my love for the game really started to blossom. I was in my second year of work with the Blackhawks Youth Hockey Camps, and those kept me super busy as well—I loved them.

Because of my major reconstructive wrist surgery, our strength and conditioning coach, Mike Boyle, who treats me like family, didn't trust me to work out independently at the Seven Bridges Ice Arena, which had been my home rink with the Chicago Mission for many years. He knew this wouldn't go over well, but he told me I would overdo it and hurt myself if I wasn't supervised. (He was right.) I relented and he contacted a local gym and sent me there.

The first day I walked in, I noticed this super big guy running shuttles, wearing a Michigan football workout shirt, and drenched in sweat. It took me a minute, but I eventually figured out he was Michael Schofield—because when I was at the Big House for the Olympic team announcement, I was reading a football team roster and saw we both went to Sandburg High School.

We shook hands and both got back to work. The next day, Michael asked me to bring my silver medal. I did. Michael and I took a picture together with it, and our first conversation stemmed from there. It didn't take long to realize how much we had in common. For one, his aunt, Coach Jane Caliendo, was my ninth-grade PE teacher.

After the picture we took ended up on the Sandburg High School Twitter page, Coach Jane commented that we should date. Michael and I followed each other on Twitter, and he DMed me an apology for his aunt's comment. I told him if he actually wanted to talk to me, he would need my phone number because I didn't want to communicate with him through social media. He loves that now because he says it was so easy to get my number, but at the time I didn't think anything of it.

Then one day he asked me if I could give him a ride to his workout. I said sure. That's when it hit me: we had lived ten minutes away from each other our whole lives and hadn't even known it. I dropped him off after the workout and he asked what I did all day.

If I had answered him honestly, it would have taken a couple of minutes, so I just said, "Nothing." I asked what he did.

"Nothing," he said. Then he asked if I'd like to do nothing together one day.

I agreed. We ended up going to a local fast-food restaurant called Pops and we were there for a few hours. His phone kept ringing with unknown numbers with zip codes from all over the country. I had no idea what was going on. It turned out the NFL scouts were calling to confirm his location and phone number in preparation for the upcoming NFL Draft and he was ignoring their calls. As soon as I found out what was going on, I insisted he answer his phone because I wasn't going to ruin his career before it even started, but I was flattered that his focus was on me on such an important day.

It didn't take us long to acknowledge the incredible synergies and similarities between us, and soon we were spending more time together. He was training for the NFL; I was working with the Blackhawks, rehabbing my wrist, making appearances, and preparing for my junior season at Northeastern University. A whole lot of nothing for the both of us!

A few weeks later the Denver Broncos drafted him in the third round, ninety-fifth pick overall, which is a pretty big deal, and Michael was on a plane to Denver at six a.m. the next day for training camp.

While we knew we weren't going to see each other much, the strong bond had already been made. We were similar in so many ways. We both had childhood dreams we were so driven to chase. Neither of us had ever been to a high school dance. We both played DI college sports. We both had close-knit families. We knew it was the real thing. While we were bummed not to be together, we weren't intimidated by the thought of being apart. I wanted him to go follow his dream and he wanted the same for me.

While my life after the Olympics had some of the highest highs—like becoming an Olympian; being greeted with so much love by so many; being able to intern with my hometown team, the Chicago Blackhawks; getting my wrist fixed; and meeting Michael and prepping for my junior year of college—it also had some of the lowest lows. Not only did we lose Bonnie that summer, when I got home from Sochi, my family let me know Grandma Coyne had fallen at the grocery store. Following her accident, her dementia went from mild to extreme and she declined quickly. She was recovering in a rehabilitation center and I went to see her and show her my new medal. While she was very forgetful and confused some of the time, she remembered me and knew exactly what my medal was for. The nurses at the rehabilitation center had turned on all my games so Grandma could watch me play, even in the middle of the night. Later that summer, on August 7, 2014, Grandma passed away. She'd visited Papa at the cemetery every day since his passing in 1998 and was finally reunited with him. She was my last grandparent, and I was very sad.

In addition, Michael's aunt, Coach Jane, had been battling stage four colon cancer hard. She was an all-around incredible woman, who had been an amazing DI coach and swimmer at the University of Illinois. She was a fighter and a warrior to the end, but unfortunately, she too lost her battle that October—though not before telling Michael and me that we were perfect for each other and that she wanted us to be together forever. Even though it wasn't under happy circumstances, that has always been so meaningful to us.

At twenty-one, I was working, trying to help my community as much as I could, and I had met someone I was pretty sure I was going to marry. So much had changed since the Olympics in February. Having a dream for so long and finally accomplishing it allowed me to take a deep breath, take a step back, and see that my Olympic dream led to a platform where I could inspire others to follow their dreams, just as I did mine. I was exhausted, but it was a good exhaustion, and I would do it all over again, if I had the opportunity. But for now, I would be heading back to Northeastern as a junior, and I was ready to get back to work as a Husky.

CHAPTER 24

CAPPING OFF COLLEGE

*One chapter's ending is the opportunity for
a new chapter's beginning—embrace it.*

I was so excited to be back for my final two years as a Husky. For one, I was looking forward to meeting the freshman and sophomore classes, who would both be brand-new to me. For another, I was more confident and experienced. I'd accomplished the dream that had consumed my life to this point. I was able to take a deep breath and lower my shoulders ten inches. There was more to life than hockey and I experienced much of it during the summer after the Olympics.

When I returned, instead of moving back into the dorms, I got a studio apartment on campus for my final two years. It was roughly the size of a napkin, but I loved it. It was amazing to have my own space, to cook for myself, and to have somewhere to recuperate at the end of my long days. I didn't need much to be happy, so I was all set.

Academically, I was still on my mission of graduating in three and a half years and starting my master's during my senior year, so

I jumped right back into a heavy schedule. As far as the team went, things were really good and I was voted captain. Our team was great, not only in terms of hockey but also as people who cared about each other and respected one another's choices, including mine of not wanting to drink alcohol even if I was of age. It felt like we were a cohesive group with a common goal: We wanted to win and we wanted to make history—together.

I had lots going on academically and professionally as well. I picked up where I left off before leaving after sophomore year, doing sideline reporting. Because the women's games were often played in the afternoon, I was available for the men's games at night. In addition, I started working in Northeastern's facilities under Facilities Manager Jack Malone. Every year, Jack would have a few students work in the office to gain valuable experience.

In order to graduate with honors in the College of Arts, Media, and Design, I would need to take an independent study course. It was no small task and required a lot of time and energy, but I was committed to doing it. I decided to examine crises in sports. Our faculty athletic representative, Professor Fred Wiseman, recommended Dr. Alan Zaremba as my independent study supervisor. Dr. Zaremba had literally written the book on crisis communication, so I had special opportunities to learn one-on-one from him. It was fascinating, stimulating, and harder than any other class I could have taken in my final undergraduate semester. I learned so much, and while it was an extra layer of work, I've always been the person who does better the more I have on my plate, so this put me at the top of my game in more ways than one.

While the work continued to pile on, Michael and I were thousands of miles away from each other but still going strong.

We weren't like some relationships I had witnessed, where the couple texted incessantly, but we were deeply bonded to each other. Neither of us wanted to distract the other. He knew I was busy, and I understood it was the same for him, so we gave each other space during the day and then really valued the time we were able to give each other on the phone at the end of the day.

A month into my senior year, which would be my final semester of undergraduate course work, I was biking back to my room from class. My phone rang. I grew concerned when I saw it was Michael, so I pumped the brakes and took the call. It turned out Michael was going to make his first career start with the Broncos in Denver that Sunday against the Minnesota Vikings. I had to be there. We played Friday and Saturday, so I knew it was possible.

I found a round-trip flight and made it in time. From that point forward, I decided I would try to be there for all the important moments in Michael's life. My vow was soon put to the test.

In February 2016, the Broncos made it to Super Bowl 50, which would be played on the opposite side of the country from Boston—in San Francisco. Right around the same time, we made it to the Beanpot Final by beating Boston University in the semifinal the Tuesday before Super Bowl Sunday, which we won 3–2. I had two goals. Beating BU never got old, especially knowing this was my last Beanpot game against them. We earned our spot in the Beanpot final, and then the Saturday before the Super Bowl we played Providence College on their home turf. Since we'd lost to them once before that season, I was laser focused on making sure we won that game.

If I was going to be at the Super Bowl, I would have to miss a practice on the eve of the Beanpot Championship. I struggled with the thought of letting my team down, but I also knew this might never happen again. Come on, it's the *Super Bowl*!

I went to Coach Flint and asked him if I could go. He told me it wasn't up to him, that it was up to my teammates; so early one morning I explained the situation. An awkward silence followed, and I started to stress. The spell was broken when our other captain, Sarah Foss, yelled out, "Can we come too?" Then everyone broke into a show of support for me.

So I rushed to grab the red-eye after our game against Providence College and get to the Super Bowl.

On February 7, 2016, Michael accomplished a childhood dream and I was there to see it. He became a Super Bowl Champion when the Broncos defeated the Carolina Panthers 24–10. We had a late night of celebrating, during which Flo Rida performed for the Broncos, and I jumped back on the plane to Boston hardly having slept, knowing I had the Beanpot Championship game as soon as I got back.

The next day we got our butts kicked by Boston College in the Beanpot final. If the game had been closer, I would have been much saltier, but they were hands down the better team that night.

At least Michael had won.

As soon as the Super Bowl parade was over, Michael flew to Boston and was there for most of the rest of the school year, and it was the best. He worked out with Mike Boyle. He came to all my games. He brought a football mentality by setting up tailgate parties before each one and drummed up support for the team. All the parents knew him. Since we didn't get to spend much time together in person, we cherished this time. He got there in February, I left in March for the IIHF Women's World Championship, and he reported back for training camp in April. But the time we didn't get together didn't matter. Of course, we missed each other like crazy! We took great care with each other and it worked out well for both of us.

Senior year was phenomenal. Part of the reason was because I finally had a healthy wrist. I got my last surgery the summer before the start of my senior year and felt like a new person. I played like it too and etched my name in history a few different ways. I finished my college career as Northeastern Women's Hockey's all-time leading goal scorer with 141 goals and all-time leading point scorer with 249; I became the all-time leading scorer in Hockey East play with 91 goals and 167 points in league games; I led the NCAA in goals with 50 that season, and I also led in goals per game, points per game, shorthanded goals, and hat tricks. I was the second Northeastern player to ever receive the Patty Kazmaier Memorial Award as the best player in Women's College Hockey, and most importantly . . .

We made the NCAA tournament.

We sat in the Cabot Center on the campus of Northeastern, with chairs and a giant projector ready to stream the NCAA selection show. We'd ended the season ranked sixth in the country, so we knew we were likely to land in the top eight and make the NCAA National Championship tournament for the first time in program history; it was just a matter of it becoming official. After making the tournament, it takes three wins to become national champions. The show kicked off and the announcer started with the eighth-ranked team and revealed it was a team from Boston— the Northeastern Huskies. It was a little anticlimactic because we had dropped from sixth to eighth, which meant our quarterfinal game would be played against the number one–seeded Boston College Eagles, who'd kicked our butts in the Beanpot final a few weeks earlier. If we were the sixth seed, we would have played the fifth seed, much better odds. Either way, we were up for the task.

We traveled five miles down the road for our first-ever NCAA tournament. The game didn't go too well; we ended up losing 5–1. With 2:40 to go, I got the puck and went end to end, took a shot, and scored. My last shift, last shot, ended with my fiftieth goal of the season; Dr. Wiedrich kept his promise of putting fifty goals in my wrist. It wasn't the way I imagined it ending, but as soon as I stepped off the ice after that goal, I knew it was the end of my journey. I would never play as a Northeastern Husky again in my life. That was hard. I'd wanted to end on top.

After my final game in a Husky jersey and after getting knocked out in the first round of the NCAA tournament, I told my team to remember the feeling of defeat and use that as motivation as they walked out of that room. We had accomplished the goal of making it to the NCAA tournament, but that *can't* be good enough.

GOLDEN COYNE

Leave everything better than you found it for those who come after you.

I had accomplished what I had come to do at Northeastern. I had helped change a program, and the team was now a contender. I started my master's degree in the final semester on campus, and by the end of the hockey season, I was ready to go. I had grown with my years, and my years had grown with me.

I left Northeastern better than I found it, and because of that many things would be better for the players who came after me. I know by the time I left Northeastern, I was satisfied I had done my part. (Of course, not winning it all left me with a little dissatisfaction.) There's always more to be done, but because of what we had accomplished, the school would provide more resources to the women's hockey program and would be able to attract high-caliber players, National Team members, as well as more Olympians, and that could only help the program continue to improve.

Northeastern has made it as far as being the second-best team in the country, with consecutive appearances in the NCAA tournament since 2018 and a runner-up performance in 2021—all under the leadership of Coach Flint. It was bittersweet leaving life on Huntington Avenue behind, knowing my time as a Husky had come to an end, but I was ready to start my new life with Michael while finishing up my master's degree.

CHAPTER 25

THE BOYCOTT

Be bold for change.

As my playing days at Northeastern came to an end, Michael was in his third season with the Broncos, so I moved to Denver to be with him. I loved it. A lot of people there appreciated being active and outside (who wouldn't when there's sunshine three hundred days a year!), which meant many were interested in health and wellness, and of course it was beautiful too, with its sharp mountain range and wide-open blue skies. The adjustment was seamless.

I did what I had always done. I got up every day to train and skate in order to keep myself in peak performance shape and be ready if and when USA Hockey called. Once I got to Denver, I asked Mike Boyle if he knew of any strength and conditioning coaches in the area, and he connected me with Loren Landow from Landow Performance, who, like Mike, is one of the best strength coaches and people I have worked with. It wasn't just Loren who was great, it was every coach and athlete in the gym. It was a family, and I had the best workout group, made up of many NFL free agents who welcomed me with open arms.

I was finishing my final semester of graduate school online. Although my five-year scholarship paid for my tuition, I was now in the real world and responsible for my living and training expenses, including rent and groceries, never mind paying strength and conditioning coaches, physical therapists, ice bills, and finding a way to afford all the other things involved with being an elite athlete. As a player on the Women's National Team, I was committed to a full-time training schedule of at least thirty hours per week. USA Hockey expected the Women's National Team players to show up fully prepared for international competitions.

USA Hockey is recognized as the national governing body (NGB) of ice hockey. As the NGB, it is responsible for training the women's teams for international competition. However, USA Hockey provided us with no financial support for our training expenses and only a nominal stipend that covered some of our expenses during the six months we were in residency leading up to the Olympics. So, like me, the majority of players had second jobs coaching and working hockey camps, and would cut deals with rink managers to get discounted ice, waking up at five a.m. to work out and skate before going to our second jobs.

I had part-time work with the Blackhawks, thanks to Annie Camins, Senior Director of Youth Hockey, who always kept me top of mind and had increased my role as a community ambassador after my work with Blackhawks Youth Hockey Camps that started in 2013. Being a DI player and a candidate for the 1998 Olympic team, Annie also understood my main focus was on my responsibilities with USA Hockey. I would make the trip from Denver to Chicago to participate in different community activities with the Blackhawks, like G.O.A.L. (Get Out and Learn) clinics, where I would introduce hockey to the students at the schools in Chicago, which was great. When I traveled into town I skated with the Chicago Mission boys' team like the good old days, worked out at the Arctic Ice Arena by myself, and stayed with my parents for free. That helped, but it didn't change the fact that as a Women's National Team player, I wasn't compensated for my worth.

USA Hockey is required by the Ted Stevens Olympic and Amateur Sports Act, a federal law, to "provide equitable support and encouragement for participation by women, where separate programs for male and female athletes are conducted on a national basis."

Basically, this means there must be gender equity. The men and boys were receiving far greater levels of support and respect. Among the many inequities, the men were provided equipment that was not made available to women, they were provided with more support staff within hockey operations and with medical staff, and USA Hockey provided championship rings to men and boys who won international championships—while I am still waiting for my championship rings from the two U18 IIHF Women's World Championships. And on the twentieth anniversary of Cammi's 1998 gold medal team, she and her teammates were still waiting for *their* rings.

The list goes on. The men often flew anything but coach while we only flew coach, oftentimes in middle seats toward the back of the plane. The men were provided single rooms while the women were given doubles. The men received $50 per diem per day, we only received $15 per day. The men were allowed to have a guest, with their transportation and lodging costs covered. This benefit was simply not provided to the women.

This unequal support was also very noticeable at the youth level. USA Hockey was spending about $3.5 million annually on its National Team Development Program (NTDP). Since 1996, the NTDP has identified and selected male hockey players under the age of eighteen and their current home base is at the USA Hockey Arena in Plymouth, Michigan. They compete in a roughly sixty-game schedule, including international tournaments. According to the information included on USA Hockey's press releases, the NTDP's goal is "to prepare student athletes under the age of eighteen for participation on US National Teams and success in their future hockey careers. Its efforts focus not only on high-caliber participation on the ice but creating well-rounded individuals off the ice."

Additionally, they were contributing $1.4 million into the United States Hockey League (USHL), an elite league for sixteen-to twenty-year-old boys. What a great opportunity for these boys. However, there is no comparable development opportunity for girls.

Our women's team had a very strong group of veteran players who had been living these inequities and saw the need for change. We were done getting treated as afterthoughts, having nothing to show for all our successes, while the boys and men who played for USA Hockey experienced a completely different level of support.

Unbeknownst to me, two of our veteran leaders, Monique and Jocelyne Lamoureux—aka the Twins—made a lifechanging and gutsy phone call. They contacted John Langel, a partner from the law firm Ballard Spahr, to explain the conditions within the Women's National Team. Ballard Spahr had a sixteen-year history working with the United States women's soccer team, so it seemed like they would be the perfect fit if they were interested.

If we were actually going to step up and take a stand and make change within USA Hockey, we would require extensive legal assistance, because at that point we had no money, no power, nothing. Generations before us had tried to make change but failed for those reasons. But everything shifted once Ballard Spahr agreed to help us. John rallied a group of partners and associates at the firm who would commit themselves to this pro bono gender-equity project. Along with John and his law partner, Diane "Dee" Spagnuolo, they sought out three associates who played sports in college and had a passion for gender equity: Kim Magrini, Ashley Wilson, and Mary Cate Gordon. It was a huge blessing since we definitely couldn't afford them. Heck, we couldn't even afford ourselves!

For postgraduate players, the conversations revolved around equitable compensation; enhanced program support; fair treatment on and off the ice; disability benefits, including pregnancy and maternity; and forming a committee to make sure we'd have a seat at the table with USA Hockey to guarantee they made the same investment in the development of girls' hockey across the United States. In addition, the committee would operate with the goal of continuing to develop opportunities for the Women's National Team from a programming, marketing, and sponsorship standpoint, as well as expand other areas within USA Hockey to ensure girls and women receive the equitable support they deserve. We refused to let the future generations of the game suffer.

Since I had left Northeastern, I was able to get up to speed on these proceedings at the IIHF Women's World Championships in Kamloops, British Columbia, in April of 2016. I had only been a postgraduate for a few hours when I arrived at that tournament and I had *a lot* to learn. Thankfully, I already had a lot of experience with the team and the veterans were great leaders and took the time to educate me step by step.

The first meeting between Ballard Spahr and USA Hockey was in Colorado Springs and took place the day after we won gold at the 2016 IIHF Women's World Championship. Nothing life-changing happened at this meeting other than an acknowledgment by USA Hockey that they had been waiting for someone to raise the issue of equitable support on behalf of the women. Consider that: they knew their obligation and yet were waiting for someone to step up to make them fulfill their duty to women. Four months then went by, and USA Hockey hadn't agreed to a second meeting.

While we were at a postgraduate camp in Boston, John and Dee flew in from Philadelphia to introduce themselves to all the players and discuss our strategy, part of which was to potentially boycott the 2017 World Championships, which were now seven months away, if USA Hockey refused to modify its ways.

It didn't shake us.

Weeks after our training camp, there was finally a second meeting in Boston. Eleven of my teammates were there along with John and Dee. USA Hockey's position was, we weren't required to train—it was our choice, and we should be grateful simply to have the opportunity to play for the Women's National Team. The message came across that even after training for thirty hours a week on our own, then working a second job, we were expected to just show up and win, with absolutely no support from USA Hockey.

We'd never felt valued or cared for, but as the weeks and months passed, dissatisfaction mounted. We knew exactly how USA Hockey felt about the Women's National Team. The things we were asking for had been provided to men's and boys' programs for years.

As we were getting closer to the 2017 World Championships—which would be held on home soil in Plymouth, Michigan, at the USA Hockey Arena, the NTDP's base—little to no progress had been made through our conversations, leaving us frustrated and exhausted. In addition, we found out our head coach, Ken Klee, had been fired. We had all figured he would be the 2018 Olympic team coach. All he did was win and he had the respect of the players. To this day, no one knows why the general manager, Reagan Carey, canned one of the most likeable and successful coaches the Women's National Team has ever had. He is still one of my favorite coaches and I am so thankful for all the time he spent developing my game and for his continued support to this day. The news that Robb Stauber, the goalie coach from the 2014 Olympic team, had been named his replacement shocked the group as much as the Ken Klee news. That was hard to swallow on top of the way we were being treated within the negotiations process. We lost our next two games, which were against Canada. Though it seemed at times USA Hockey was trying to defeat us, they couldn't.

When there was another meeting in Denver in February 2017, I went along with the Twins and Dee and Mary Cate from the Ballard team. It took every ounce of strength not to show my anger as USA Hockey went on and on, making it clear we should be grateful to have an opportunity and a team to play on. Thinking about all the sacrifice, commitment, and dedication I had put into USA Hockey since I was fifteen years old, along with my teammates' work, I couldn't believe we were being so undervalued.

On March 15, 2017, we were six days from our World

Championship pre-camp and had two weeks until our first game. USA Hockey did not see what was coming next, and boy oh boy was it powerful. We announced that we would be boycotting the World Championship until significant progress was made.

It shocked USA Hockey but it also shocked the world. Every major news outlet picked up the story and the public support was incredible and uplifting. Our hashtag #BeBoldForChange was trending everywhere. ESPN was always on at Landow Performance. People would periodically scan the highlights and breaking news on the bottom line. On the scroll it read, "US WOMEN'S NATIONAL HOCKEY TEAM TO BOYCOTT THE WORLD CHAMPIONSHIPS DUE TO STALLED CONTRACT NEGOTIATIONS." I walked into the gym and was mobbed by questions from my workout partners. People wanted to know if that was my team and asked the details of how we got treated. There was more of a reaction than we had anticipated, and it was exhilarating but also exhausting.

True to who they were, instead of trying to come to some kind of agreement, USA Hockey began trying to replace our roster with as many American-born women's hockey players as possible: DI players, DIII players, and even high school players, offering what for some was the chance of a lifetime. But we had anticipated their move and had already started to call all those college players, high school players, and their coaches to educate them that this fight was beyond the twenty-three players on the world championship team. It was a fight against USA Hockey's inequitable treatment of all girls and women in the sport. It was about all of us and the generations to come.

Not one player agreed to play.

Not one, and USA Hockey called a lot of players.

After all players said no, our one voice only grew stronger, and I knew at that point USA Hockey was in trouble.

Four days later, USA Hockey requested a meeting with us, which was momentous since we had always been the ones trying to get their attention. A small group of veteran players flew to Philadelphia to meet with USA Hockey at a time when we were supposed to be at training camp preparing for the World Championship. When we got to the Ballard Spahr offices, it was a scene. I felt like I was in a movie. Our lawyers tried to cover our faces as we passed the clicking and flashing cameras while the local news attempted to get our attention for comment.

We were in that room for twelve long hours, while the rest of the players were back home on their phones listening in the *entire* time. Back and forth, back and forth. While it was grueling, by the end of it we felt pretty good about what we'd put on the table and were hopeful they had heard us. The day was longer than expected and many of us missed our flights. We woke up in the morning to find out they were still reaching out to replacement players. Twelve hours of conversation had all come to . . . nothing? Meanwhile, all this time we should have been at training camp and now we had less than a week until we were supposed to be opening up against Canada. Players were still scrambling to commit to their training in case we did play. Some were on the ice with headphones in their ears, phones tucked away in their hockey pants, listening to calls since we were on our phones just about every hour of the day for those two weeks. I remember charging my phone twice in a day and at one point having to leave workouts at Loren's so I could field calls.

People reached out to offer support, like the players' associations from the WNBA, NHL, MLB, NFL, and NBA. Icons like Billie Jean King and Cammi Granato were behind us. Twenty United States senators wrote a letter to USA Hockey demanding that we receive equitable support. Due to the power of those supporting us, on a Monday night, four days before the World Championships were set to begin, USA Hockey called an emergency board meeting with their ninety-one-person board to approve or deny the deal, as it had to be unanimous. Thankfully, Julie Chu and Meghan Duggan were on the board and had a moment to have the floor and explain our fight, that this wasn't just about money, that we weren't being greedy, that we were asking to be treated fairly; to explain this wasn't about twenty-three players, this was about equitable treatment from USA Hockey. They explained the many things the men and boys had received for years and the things the girls and women had never received. I wasn't on that call but know their voice and leadership in that moment really helped determine our fate.

> **GOLDEN COYNE**
>
> *A unified voice willing to risk everything will lead to necessary change for future generations.*

We all stood by our phones and waited to hear the results of the board meeting.

On Tuesday, March 28, 2017, the deal was signed.

We had done it.

The players and the game got what they deserved.

First thing Wednesday morning, we were all on flights from our respective homes to Detroit. As the team began to gather there was a moment of relief, as well as a hug filled with joy, pride, and exhaustion. We had fought long and hard and it had all been worth it.

By Friday, we were playing in the opening game of the tournament. We knew we had to win the World Championship to prove our worth once again. Ten days after we signed the deal, we were throwing our gloves in the air as my teammate, Hilary Knight, scored the game-winning goal in overtime to secure a 3–2 win over Canada in the gold medal game in front of a sold-out crowd in Plymouth, Michigan. It was downright poetic. It was my favorite World Championship for so many reasons. My family was able to be there; Michael was there; his mom, Kath, and dad, Mike (Michael is a III), were there; Bosko was there; and once again Michael brought the football tailgating mentality to hockey. Being on home soil, we had so many families and friends in attendance, many there for moral support after everything we had just been through. I tied for the tournament lead with twelve points, five goals, and seven assists, with the most important assist coming on Hilary's game-winner.

People all around us cheered the team on, and little girls and their parents held up signs that said THANK YOU FOR BEING BOLD #BEBOLDFORCHANGE. Parents and kids in autograph lines thanked us for being bold. I remember seeing a sign a girl was holding saying thank you and getting teary-eyed, for many reasons. For one I was dead tired, but I had hope that little girl would never be told she had no value the way I had by USA Hockey. It felt like we had made a significant step for girls and women in the sport of hockey. We knew it was about so much more than the game but as always there was still so much more work to be done.

CHAPTER 26

GOING FOR GOLD

*Don't forget your roots, who you are,
or who helped you get there.*

*I*n May 2017, I flew to Tampa Bay, Florida, to try out for the Women's National Team in hopes of earning a spot on the Olympic team. USA Hockey had invited forty-one players for a week-long tryout in hopes of earning a spot on the 2018 Olympic team, and unlike in previous years, after the tryout we had individual meetings to find out if we made it or not. They picked twenty-three players right then and there in May, including me. You can imagine how extra elated we were when our general manager, Reagan Carey, told us we'd made the team and the fear of getting cut throughout the residency months was eliminated. We wouldn't have to be part of that awful reality show again, watching people's dreams cut short without warning. Instead, we could focus on the task at hand, bond as a team, and get ready for the Olympics. All we had to do was put in the work and be the best we could be every day.

During the first week of September, the twenty-three of us

were to report to Tampa for residency. At that time, local residents were evacuating because of Hurricane Irma, while I flew in as the hurricane was approaching. There was almost no one on the plane and I was surprised it was flying at all given the weather warnings. But our general manager and coaches wanted us to start on time, so on time we were. We were concerned, and our loved ones were concerned. I arrived at my room, and almost immediately my teammates and I were evacuated to a large ballroom for safety. We slept on the pool floats they gave us, and were advised to bring our hockey helmets for protection. This was a disastrous start to residency—pun intended—and gave us a taste of the kind of hard year it was going to be.

At the end of October, we played Canada in Boston and played poorly. The physical and mental demands of residency made it hard to be sharp. After our loss, our GM announced that she was bringing in defensemen Cayla Barnes, a freshman from Boston College, as a contender for the Olympic team. The landscape quickly changed as we realized someone was going to get cut.

A few weeks later we played in the Four Nations Cup and hosted the tournament at our home rink in Tampa. Even with all the difficulties, we ended up playing Canada in the final, beating them 5–1 and winning a third consecutive Four Nations Cup. I led the team in the tournament with four goals and three assists in four games. It was one of my best performances because I controlled what I could control and let everything else go so I could play my best game. Sure, I was worried I was going to get cut, but I knew if I did everything I could, no matter what happened, I'd have no regrets.

After winning the Four Nations Cup with a 4–0 record, we

were surprised with two no-puck practices in a row. A practice with no pucks means a bag skate, which means an extremely difficult, exhausting, and miserable practice. There were puke buckets, players on the verge of passing out, and many pulled groins. Two of the three coaches didn't even come on the ice, and instead stood on the bench with whistles. The team had been through so much and we were reaching a breaking point.

Thankfully, we finally had some time off, and I was on my way to the airport to get on a cross-country flight to LA to see Michael, who was now playing for the LA Chargers after three seasons in Denver. I didn't care if I was traveling twelve hours for only three days with him. If I didn't get away, I was going to lose it. En route to the airport, our general manager sprang a conference call on the team. We were told that two additional players would be coming in, which meant two more of us would be cut.

We now had twenty-six players and had to get down to twenty-three. Families had already bought tickets to South Korea since we had been told in May this was the team, but now everyone stopped making plans. We had a couple more pre-Olympic tour games, and we all knew every one of us were potentially on the chopping block. Finally, they cut three of the players who had been told they had made the team and our twenty-three-person roster was set.

The final team was announced at the 2018 NHL Winter Classic, but this time we didn't attend as a team. They simply announced the roster during intermission, and shortly after we flew from Tampa to Atlanta and then to Seoul to go through processing. When we got to the Olympic Village, this time I was excited to experience everything I could. Our coaches left it up to us whether we wanted to go to opening ceremonies or not and it was a no-brainer. We were going. The first day we got to Pyeongchang I got drug tested, and had to give both blood and urine. It was horrible. They had difficulty drawing blood and it made me feel nauseous.

We opened up the tournament two days later against Finland. For the three years leading up to the Olympics, I had been on a line with center Decks and right winger Hilary, which was one of the most dominant lines in women's hockey history. A month before the Olympics, Robb shuffled the lines, so I was with a different line.

In the first period we went down 1–0 to Finland, and all of a sudden I was back on a line with Decks and Hilary. In that game I got a backdoor pass from Hilary and buried it bar-down on Noora Räty, one of the best goaltenders to ever play the game. Not only was I happy to give our team the lead, but similar to how I felt after all my victories against BU, this backdoor goal was extra special since Robb had been the one trying to make me do the eye program in 2014, specifically because he thought I couldn't score backdoor goals.

We had two days off between each preliminary game. We beat Russia 5–0 and then lost to Canada 2–1. I scored a nifty goal in that game, but one wasn't enough. We had four days between the preliminary round and the semifinal game we would play against Finland. During those four days, I went to see figure skating events, short-track speed skating, as well as the men's hockey games. My favorite event was seeing Maia and Alex Shibutani, the brother-sister ice dancing duo, win a bronze medal for Team USA. If my teammates and I weren't at the events, we were hanging out with the other athletes in the Olympic Village, watching Team USA compete on TV, and getting ready for our upcoming game.

We beat Finland 5–0 in the semifinal. We had made it to the gold medal game.

The moment I remember best leading up to the gold medal game was when Cammi Granato surprised us on FaceTime to wish us good luck. As soon as we got off the phone with her, I thought, *We're going to win.*

February 22, 2018 finally came, a date we'd had marked on our calendars for a long, long time.

Some of us had waited four years for revenge, others didn't know what it was like to lose a game like this. That was the strength of our group. We had Olympic rookies that didn't play like rookies. They only knew what it felt like to win, and their confidence was contagious.

On the day of the game we woke up early and did a warm-up with our strength and conditioning coach Jim Radcliffe. From there we had a meal and then it was time.

GOLDEN COYNE

In the big moments, don't let the highs get too high or the lows get too low. Stay composed. Lean on each other. Support each other. And most importantly, have fun and enjoy the moment.

I've never played in an uneventful gold medal game. This was no exception. We were down 2–1 until Monique scored with 6:21 left in the third period to tie the game, thanks to an incredible stretch pass by Kelly Pannek to send Monique on a breakaway. The game was tied at two and the last six minutes were constant back and forth action. When the buzzer hit zero, we went back into the locker room for an intermission, then into a twenty-minute four-on-four overtime . . and we were still tied. Next up was a five-player shootout. We hadn't worked on shootouts all year; in fact, it wasn't until we got to South Korea that Alex (Rigsby) Cavallini, one of our goaltenders, asked Robb if we could. Thank goodness she asked.

We were still tied after five shootout rounds and went into a sixth. Jocelyne scored on one of the most impressive shootout moves I have ever seen. I was even more impressed that she was able to do that move under the highest stakes and pressure in the entire sport. She didn't show an ounce of stress, just nerves of steel through her famous "Oops, I did it again" move, which was what she called it after the fact. It was jaw-dropping. Seriously. YouTube it.

Our twenty-year-old goaltender Maddie Rooney, who was only five months old when the 1998 team won gold, was as cool as a cucumber when Meghan Agosta came up for a second time after scoring for Canada in an earlier round. Rooney came up big and made the save.

We won.

History was made.

The twenty-year wait was over.

Our team overcame and conquered. It was the most amazing feeling in the world, standing locked arm in arm, listening to our national anthem, seeing the American flag raised higher than everyone else's as Olympic champions. We belted our anthem proudly and then searched the crowd for our families, our supporters, the ones who had gotten us through this difficult year.

Once again, my whole family was there and had enjoyed their

time as experienced Olympic Games attenders. While I didn't see them that much because they were having such a good time, it was a lot more than in 2014! After we won gold, Michael led the charge onto the ice and my teammates' families followed. I took a picture with my family, and then Michael lifted me into the air, my gold medal dangling between us. When I got back to the Olympic Village, I had a text that took my breath away and brought tears to my eyes. It was a moment everything came full circle for me.

A message from Cammi.

She had taken the time to reach out in the middle of the night to congratulate me for winning the gold, telling me how proud she was. She inspired a generation of girls to believe there was a place for them in this sport—receiving that text from her with a gold medal around my neck at the Olympic Games was the proof she did just that.

The whole night was awesome and that really capped it off.

When we got home, the response was overwhelming. We went on a post-Olympic tour. We flew into LA to be on *The Ellen Show* and to be honored at an LA Kings game, then to Tampa to drop off our stuff from the Olympics and attend a Tampa Bay Lightning game, then to Washington, DC, to be honored at the Stadium Series game at the Naval Academy in Annapolis. This stop held a little extra significance for me, because forty-eight hours after we won gold, Jake had to report to Fort Gordon, Georgia, as a commissioned officer in the United States Army, as a member of the cyber command. I will forever be grateful for all our service men and women and their families who have served and continue to serve our country.

We then went to New York for numerous appearances including *Late Night with Jimmy Fallon* and events hosted by the New York Rangers and New Jersey Devils. From there it was back to Tampa before *finally* going home, a day many of us were ready for. A few weeks later we were also recognized at the Team USA Awards for Olympic Team of the Year and at ESPN's ESPY Awards for Best Game of that year. Going to the ESPYs was a surreal moment but winning an ESPY was even better. It was eye-opening, because for so long we were told that no one cared about women's hockey. Turns out, lots of people did. Once again, we had proved people wrong.

It was like the whole world was finally seeing our value and reflecting our worth back to us. The Olympics is a huge platform where people can see women's hockey. They saw the skill, the speed, the talent necessary to play the game at the highest level. They saw how hard we worked while balancing second jobs. People were able to understand why we had fought for what we had the year before and wanted to hear our stories. We said we had worth and then we proved it. But moments like these also showcased why we need women's hockey to be visible more than every four years. The talent is there every day but the platform to witness it is not.

It was so fun to see how my teammates' hometowns were celebrating them too. Palos Heights outdid itself and celebrated even harder this time. They gave me the key to the city, and I got to be the grand marshal of the Fourth of July parade. I made more appearances, talked to even more schools, went to more events, and I continued coaching at the Blackhawks Youth Hockey Camps, which was especially wonderful because many of the kids who'd already seen my silver medal were extra elated to see my new gold medal. In addition, the Kendall Coyne Hockey Camp I started in 2016 really boomed. I had over one hundred girls from all over the United States come to the camp to be on the ice where it all started for me in Orland Park, Illinois. I knew exactly how those kids felt; I had been them twenty years earlier. It's so hard to explain how it feels to wear that gold medal for the first time, but I get to relive it every time I see the wonder on a kid's face when it goes around their neck or is held in their hand. That summer I was the only woman who played in the Chicago Pro Hockey League, a summer league made up of professional players who reside in Chicago. The associate head coach of the Rockford Ice Hogs, Anders Sorensen, was a longtime coach of the Chicago Mission Boys and always welcomed me to skate with his teams. He knew I could play alongside the men in this league and that it would be a great summer training opportunity. Little did he know, so many young hockey players would fill the stands with signs that had my name on it. It was fun playing against players like Patrick Kane and with a player like Connor Murphy. I had eight goals and five assists in five games.

I was inducted into the Chicagoland Sports Hall of Fame, which was a wonderful honor. The Plush Horse, where Michael proposed to me on January 14, 2017, named an ice cream after me called the Golden Coyne. I threw out the first pitch for a second time at a Chicago White Sox game. (Well, throw is a stretch; I brought my hockey stick and shot the baseball off the mound. Since I threw the ball in 2014, I wanted to get creative.) Dad was so happy I finally made it to the big leagues, playing his favorite sport, but I somehow found a way to bring hockey into it. The Blackhawks honored me, which was extra special. Alex (Rigsby) Cavallini was with me and we were in full equipment as we stepped onto the United Center ice for a slow lap, a standing ovation, a USA chant, and a puck drop with Patrick Kane from the Blackhawks and Brian Gionta from the Boston Bruins, both United States Olympians. It's a Chicago tradition to cheer and clap during the national anthem and we stood there while everyone sang and cheered. It still gives me chills when I think of it. It was truly the moment of a lifetime.

Still, sometimes when you think you've reached the end, it's really only the beginning of something else.

CHAPTER 27

HAPPILY EVER AFTER

Find your teammate for life.

D uring the wild Olympic residency year in Tampa, my escape
from the difficult training environment was planning my
wedding. When I got home from the Olympics, there were so
many celebrations happening, but there was nothing I was looking forward to more than the honor I would have on July 7, 2018:
marrying my best friend.

We didn't have many options since there were only two weeks
in July that worked with our schedules. The Olympics ended in
February, Michael had OTAs (organized team activities) in April
through the end of June, and then Michael returned for training
camp and the hockey season started in August. It really was the
only time. I loved the date too; the number 77 held so much significance to me since that was Liz's number, and the number 7 was
always my favorite because of Chris Chelios. It was meant to be.

You can probably guess by now I wasn't the type of girl who
had been dreaming of her wedding since childhood. The thought
of wearing a dress never excited me, but on this day, it did.

We got married surrounded by family and friends at St. Michael's Church in Orland Park, followed by a reception in Oak Brook, Illinois. Bailey was my maid of honor, and Bosko and Michael's four sisters—Nikki, Stephanie, Kathleen, and Jackie—were all bridesmaids. Gusty and Callen, my billet siblings who I lived with in 2014, were juniors in the wedding. Mackenzie did a reading at the ceremony and so did Michael's aunt Mary. Michael's brother Andrew was the best man, his cousin Shane and best friend, Ben, along with Kevin and Jake, were groomsmen. Michael's brothers-in-law Scott and Marty were ushers, and his Nana and Papa walked down the aisle together. At my request, Jake wore his army dress uniform for the ceremony. It was perfect.

When we first went to look at the reception hall, there was a tree out front with a giant sign bearing the words THE OHIO BUCK-EYE TREE. If there is one thing Michael loves more than me and his family, it's the University of Michigan, and there's nothing stronger than the rivalry between Michigan and Ohio State. Okay, okay, maybe the one between the United States and Canada in women's hockey, but we're on the same level. As soon as we turned the corner and he saw the sign and the tree, he grabbed my hand and said, "This isn't the one."

I said, "No way, we can't bail because of the tree! We have an appointment, and they are expecting us."

Well, guess where we wound up having our reception? That's right. It was the perfect place for us, and you better believe when the day came, we put a giant maize-and-blue, block-M University of Michigan flag over the sign, which was arranged so people could just see what was under it. Michael has his limits.

I am surprised he didn't make me defriend Bosko because she is a Buckeye!

The day was so special. The morning of the wedding, the doorbell rang; Michael had sent me flowers with a card that read I CAN'T WAIT TO MARRY YOU. While everyone oohed and aahed around me, I totally panicked. I hadn't thought to send him anything. The makeup artist asked me what gifts we'd gotten each other, and I was like, *I was supposed to get him something?* I'd never done this before, and I didn't know what the rules were. Meanwhile, he'd gone and done something so sweet.

We had planned the liturgy for the ceremony, and had a pianist, trumpet player, and violin player performing "One Step Closer" as I walked down the aisle.

As the ceremony began, my dad and I locked arms and looked at each other.

"Are you nervous?" I asked him.

"Yeah, I'm nervous," he said.

"Why?" I asked.

"This is a big moment!"

"Yeah, but it's not like I'm making the wrong decision! It's not like we have to win anything!" I told him. Even though I said that, I was overwhelmed with nerves too.

Then, apparently, when they opened the church doors for my grand entrance, I basically tore off toward Michael. Dad now says I didn't walk down the aisle, I *ran*. I guess I wouldn't be me if I hadn't, but if there was one moment in my life I wished I hadn't gone so fast, it was that one. I loved the music, and we didn't get to hear all of it because I was already at the altar!

Michael's family is huge, so we had a big wedding. Late into the night cheeseburgers were brought out and we sang "Cheeseburgers in Paradise." We also had The Plush Horse there as well (of course), and the line for ice cream was hopping all night.

One thing I can say about Michael and me from all our years of having to be totally present for sports is that we've learned how to be in the moment, and we really appreciated every second of that day. I don't remember touching my cell phone once or having a worry in the world. Everything and everyone I wanted was there in that moment. We felt so lucky to have all our family and friends around us. We made our wedding exactly what we wanted it to be. And one thing we'd really wanted was our parents to enjoy themselves and not to have to work—to be able to attend and relax, and be on the receiving end of our gratitude for the myriad ways they had supported us and helped us get to where we were.

GOLDEN COYNE

Enjoy the moment.

I think we achieved that goal, and I'm so glad.

It was a truly perfect day, and when I look back now, it was the last day I can think of when I was only worried about me, Michael, and my family. I'm so happy we got to have that one-day break.

14.346 SECONDS LATER

Seize the moment.

The 2019 NHL All-Star Weekend was held in San Jose, California. My longtime teammate Brianna Decker and I were invited by the NHL as two players from Team USA, alongside two players from Team Canada, Renata Fast and Rebecca Johnston. We were there to represent the women's game on this major platform. We knew it was a huge opportunity because the women's game desperately needed more recognition and visibility. Everyone knows where to go to find their favorite NHL team and player, but when it comes to the women's game and players, people scratch their heads.

Before heading to the event, we had a call with the NHL to establish what skills each of us would be demonstrating for the fans attending the skills competition. We came to the conclusion that Renata and I would be handling the accuracy-shooting competition; Decks would be doing the premier passer, which was really tough—and no one wanted to do it, so major props to her for volunteering; and then Rebecca would be doing the puck control race. We would also have fan engagements and signings over the weekend. In addition, the NHL asked us if we would be interested in assisting the event staff during the rehearsal for the skills competition, and we all said yes.

I was the last of the four of us to arrive. I got there at five fifteen and rehearsal started at six o'clock. Patrick Burke, the senior director of player safety at the NHL and the one in charge of the on-ice components of the NHL All-Star Skills Competition, greeted me and immediately said if I got my equipment on fast enough, I could rehearse the Fastest Skater Competition for fun since none of us were demonstrating it the following day . . or at least we thought.

Patrick has been around hockey his whole life and he knew my speed was elite enough to keep up with the men, so he thought it would be fun to see what my time would be during the rehearsal. I did too. In 2007, I had watched Andy McDonald fill in for Henrik Zetterberg and he ended up winning the Fastest Skater Competition. Andy was a smaller player, undrafted, and had been proving people wrong his whole career. After watching him skate, I always thought it would be so cool to be able to try that one day, but never saw anything like it in women's hockey. This would probably be my one and only opportunity to skate the laser-timed course other than my on-ice conditioning tests with USA Hockey, which were definitely not this fun, so I was excited.

Back to the rush of the rehearsal. The Fastest Skater Competition is first, so when I walked into San Jose's SAP Center, the first skater during the rehearsal was about to start. USA Hockey shipped our jerseys and socks to the arena, and when I asked for mine, it turned out a sock was missing, so I just started getting dressed. Meanwhile, I was literally moments away from being needed on the ice if I wanted to rehearse fastest skater and I was still without a sock. The USA Hockey media coordinator who was supposed to have my socks brought in a little kid's sock and dangled it in the air in front of me as the solution.

I said, "This is no joke. That is not going to fit. Where's my hockey sock?"

He said, "I have no idea. I'm going to have to call the USA Hockey offices and have another one shipped here tomorrow."

That was not helpful given the time constraints. At that point, I was ready to go out with one sock.

Thankfully, Renata Fast had an extra pair of socks in her bag, which she loaned me. It's a funny thing being competitors one day and companions the next, but she really came through just in time for me to sprint onto the ice.

Patrick asked me if I was warm, and I said it was as good as it was going to get (the real answer—no, I was not warm. I had just gotten off a four-hour flight forty-five minutes prior!) and I was up on the red line immediately, as I made it just in time to be the last skater before they had to switch to the next event. The ref blew the whistle and I skated my hot lap. It was fun. I scored a time of 14.226 seconds. I had nothing to compare it to other than players' old scores in the past and really didn't think anything of it, other than it was fun to be able to do the lap, because I love going fast and why not get a time.

Ray Whitney and Shane Doan—two longtime, now-retired NHL players—were coaching that weekend and were also on the ice helping for the rehearsal. When I skated through the red line, they turned to Patrick and said, "Wow, she can beat some of the guys! Why isn't she doing this tomorrow?"

Patrick, who has been a fan of mine since seeing me play in the 2014 Olympics, abruptly responded, "Yeah, I've been trying to tell you all that!"

That seemed to be that. We rehearsed the other events, which was a blast. The night went on and we proceeded with the schedule we had. Meanwhile, the Colorado Avalanche's Nathan MacKinnon—who was scheduled to skate in the Fastest Skater Competition—had taken a puck to the foot the night before. The news broke that he wouldn't be able to skate. There are eight players in the competition and now they had a choice: run it with seven or pick someone to replace him.

Patrick tore into action. He'd had this vision for a long time and knew it would be a gigantic moment for the game. He took my rehearsal time to Gary Bettman, the commissioner of the NHL. It was a time that would have placed sixth a year prior in Tampa.

"Look," he said, "Nathan can't skate. Kendall can."

"Do you think she can do it?" Gary asked.

"Absolutely!" Patrick said.

"Great. You need to get it approved by the NHLPA [players' association] and the players scheduled to skate because there is prize money. We need to make sure the NHL players will be okay with a non-NHLPA player getting the money if she wins. But, if you get their approval, let's do it."

That was just what Patrick wanted to hear. He got the NHLPA's approval and all of the competing players except one, who happened to be at the Apple Store because his phone had broken. Time was of the essence, and this was a very exciting prospect since no woman had ever competed in any capacity before. That player got life back in his phone and he agreed.

In fact, it was widely believed that no woman *could* compete with men's times in the Fastest Skater Competition, so there would be no point in opening it up to women. But Patrick believed in me, he believed in us. He thought I could do it and he rallied support.

January 25, 2019 was a quiet morning with a few fan engagement activities, until my phone rang. I didn't answer it because I didn't recognize the number.

It rang again. I didn't answer again.

Then I got a text from Patrick saying, *KENDALL, IT'S PATRICK. CALL ME.*

I immediately did so, and Patrick said, "You are going be the first woman to compete in the NHL All-Star Skills Competition. You need anything? You need food? You need water? You feel good?"

I told him I was good and then sat on my bed and took a deep breath.

After that things moved so quickly. I barely had time to think. Officially, on Twitter the Avalanche asked if I would take Nathan's spot and I responded, "It would be my honor! I'll get to the rink as fast as I can." Pun intended.

This was only moments after Patrick had told me.

I spoke to Mom, Michael, and Bosko to tell them what was about to happen and that they should watch. Michael tried everything he could to get a flight from Chicago to San Jose in time to be there, but it was too short notice. Of course he'd lived in LA for three years, and the one moment he wasn't in LA was the most crucial (I would argue). I couldn't reach Dad, who could go hours without his phone. I knew he'd be on the train home from the city at that time and I didn't want him to miss it. The Fastest Skater

Competition was first, and I was the first of the first, the literal opener of the entire event.

First event.

First up.

First woman.

No pressure.

When we arrived at the rink, Renata, Rebecca, Decks, and I walked the red carpet together, which was thrilling, and then the rink was mayhem. The fact I would be competing was huge news, so after the red carpet I was running from interview to interview—everything from the NHL Network to NBC Sports to news channels in between—while also trying to get somewhat prepared for the event itself. After all, I'd been skating my whole life and I'd always been fast. In some ways I had been preparing for this since I first stepped onto the ice and learned how much I loved to go that fast.

After all the jazz, I had fifteen minutes to get ready and then it was time for the on-ice warm-ups. There was one problem: I wasn't sure if I was allowed since no one told me, and I don't think the NHL knew either. So I asked if I could go onto the ice.

Patrick came over the walkie-talkie. "Of course she is! She is opening the show! Let her out!"

Taking warm-ups without a helmet like the old days, I shot a puck at all-time great New York Ranger goaltender Henrik Lundquist, and just kept telling myself not to hit him in the head. Even though I wasn't doing anything that incorporated pucks that evening, I couldn't resist taking a shot on him. I really wanted to keep the puck afterward. It was just all so cool.

When warm-ups ended, Patrick Kane came up to me and said, "You got this, have fun."

I appreciated his reassurance since we had skated together before and he knew I what I could do. Somehow after warm-ups, I ended up in the Pacific Division locker room to wait while the ice was getting cut. Goaltender Marc-Andre Fleury, of the Vegas Golden Knights at the time and current Chicago Blackhawk, came up to introduce himself. I obviously knew who he was, but his doing so was a testament to everything I had always heard about his amazing character and class. It then turned out I wasn't allowed in that locker room and got booted.

Thankfully, Patrick showed up and walked me to the opposite side of the rink, where the other three women were. I was so fearful I would lose an edge from walking around the entire concourse without skate guards on. All it takes is stepping on some dirt, sand, candy, popcorn, a penny, you name it—anything other than rubber or ice—to lose an edge and not be able to turn without falling. This would have been an awful time for my edges to be compromised in any way, and I already knew they weren't in the best shape because I didn't get them sharpened before I arrived and I wasn't about to ask. Heck, I didn't even bring my elbow pads because I didn't think I would need those either! I knew it was out of my control at this point and I needed to stop worrying about it.

In terms of the competition, the difference between first and eighth place is usually under a second. Connor McDavid, of the Edmonton Oilers, is insanely fast and had won it two years in a row. He was going for his third consecutive victory. I accepted I probably wouldn't be first, but I needed a clean run and of course I really hoped not to be last. I knew I could not fall or stumble. As the first woman ever to do this, every stride I took would be under a microscope. If I caught an edge or stumbled at all, the pundits would say, "I told you so. Girls and women don't belong here. She can't even skate in a circle." And take the game back years.

Then it was time. I took a deep breath and told myself the advice I give to others: *believe in yourself*, skate like you have been skating your whole life, and move your legs as fast as they can go. When I heard my name called, I skated up to the red line, crouched down, and then stood back up when the whole SAP Center, majority being San Jose Shark fans, started chanting, "USA! USA! USA!" The ref started the countdown: thirty seconds, twenty seconds. I could barely hear him because of the crowd. All I could think about were my teammates. I wished they could all be there with me.

I got back into my starting position and the countdown ended, the whistle blew, and I took off as hard and as fast as I could.

It was over so fast.

14.346 seconds.

I looked up at my time and was immediately disappointed because my rehearsal time had been 14.226 seconds. Either way, in those 14.346 seconds, people had seen that a woman could skate as fast as a man. I high-fived all the players who were standing on the bench, so excited for me and my performance. I was nervous and thrilled to watch the other skaters take their turns.

Miro Heiskanen, who went right after me, fell and thankfully was okay. He wasn't allowed to go back to the starting line but did anyway and went again. All I thought was, thank goodness that wasn't me. There were no do-overs for me; it was the unspoken double standard of the moment. Clayton Keller went third and got 14.526 seconds, and right away Patrick Kane tapped my arm and said, "You beat one of 'em so far." The next five skaters were Elias Pettersson of the Vancouver Canucks, Cam Atkinson of the Columbus Blue Jackets, Jack Eichel of the Buffalo Sabres, Mathew Barzal of the New York Islanders, and the soon-to-be three-time champ Connor McDavid. McDavid, one of the greatest hockey players the game has ever seen, won with a time of 13.378 seconds. I was .968 of a second off his time, which I was pleased with.

I couldn't have anticipated what came after the event. No one could. The response was explosive. Thousands and thousands of messages from girls and boys around the world skating their own laps, people saying they never saw a girl or woman play hockey, girls saying they never saw anyone who looked like them, so many girls who now wanted to play hockey too. Hundreds of media requests came in from around the world. I thought the 2018 Olympic win had been the pinnacle, but it was nothing compared to this, at least for me personally. I had won as a team before, but this became a personal highpoint that put me in the limelight in a whole different way.

This was a chance to prove perceptions wrong, not just for those currently in the game but for all of those who would come after. We have fought so hard for so long to shatter narratives around gender. We've put a product on the ice that has showcased how fast, skilled, and talented we are. We were done being referred to as "women in hockey," which somehow made us feel less-than. We were hockey players, end of story, no further description needed. There's still a wow factor every time we do well because people aren't used to seeing what we can do other than every four years at the Olympic Games. Oftentimes, people view us as an event that comes and goes when we deserve to be more than that—a consistent presence for the sport of hockey.

Truth is, I was in the right place at the right time. What if Nathan MacKinnon hadn't been hit with that puck the day before? What if my flight had been delayed by minutes and I'd missed the rehearsal? What if Patrick hadn't advocated to get women involved at the NHL All-Star Weekend? But most of all, that moment would never have happened without all the players who have worked so hard to prove the skill and talent in women's hockey over the last twenty years.

We need more allies like Patrick Burke in life, who challenges the status quo, speaks up, and stands up for equality. He believed in us when no one else did, and he created more believers from that moment. I will be forever grateful for the fact that he went the extra mile, said I could do it, and then went the extra-*extra* mile to make sure it actually came to fruition. Because of what he facilitated, impact was made both on the sport of hockey and the role of women within its boundaries.

When the Fastest Skater Competition had ended and was successful just like Patrick knew it would be, I gave him a huge hug, and saw him pull his mic to his mouth and say to his team, "I told you so."

Not only did I leave San Jose with a lifetime of memories, I bought one souvenir—a 2019 NHL All-Star Nathan MacKinnon T-shirt. I thought it would be fitting.

The next night, all four women were offered Adidas contracts to represent the first-ever women's hockey team at the company. It was yet another realm in which I could show myself to be a pioneer, and Adidas also agreed to outfit my hockey camp and provide the girls with the resources they needed to participate. The benefit to others was more important than any benefit to myself. This game had brought me so many incredible things; it was my turn to use my platform resources and voice to ensure the future generation of players had even more.

My life exploded with emails, messages, mail, appearances, speeches, and interview requests, hearing from so many people how that moment changed their life too. NBC Sports asked me to broadcast a game a few days later. I joined John Forslund, Eddie Olczyk, and Pierre McGuire for the game in Pittsburgh. I was thankful Eddie was there, who also hails from Palos Heights, to provide me with advice in this big moment. One game turned into another. I then became the second woman ever to serve as an analyst for an NHL playoff game on NBC Sports, joining Kenny Albert and Pierre McGuire. It was special to call a game alongside Kenny, not only because he is a Hall of Famer, but he called our gold medal game and the skate at the All-Star Skills Competition, so I always tell Kenny he has been there for the biggest moments of my life—he just missed the wedding! I also began working with NHL Network. The experience I'd sought out as a sideline reporter at Northeastern was starting to pay off.

While the response was incredible, it was another moment that proved how important visibility is. I had been skating like this my whole life, but because of the platform I had skated on at the NHL All-Stars Skill Competition, more people saw my abilities. Some said they'd never seen a girl or woman skate like that before or seen a ponytail on the ice. I got thank yous from companies in the mail because their sales went up when I skated by their logos on the rinkboards. I even got recognized in the airport upon my arrival back into Chicago.

Truly surreal.

A few short weeks later, thanks to our fight for more programming during the 2017 boycott, the National Team was scheduled to play in the newly established Rivalry Series. This meant three games against Team Canada, with two games in Canada and one in the United States. After All-Star Weekend, ticket sales were booming.

While I was tired from all the appearances and interviews, playing in front of huge crowds was exactly what we deserved. I knew that moment made an impact. At one point, multiple players came up to me on the bus when we were in Toronto and said, "You have to see this!" It was a four-year-old's mom reaching out to me with a video on social media. Her daughter was skating her own lap with a message saying she wanted to be just like me. I saw it and beamed, and so did my teammates. That video meant everything to us. The young girl who once never wanted to play hockey because she thought it was only for her brother now knew it was for her too, and started playing hockey. A day later we played Team Canada at the Scotiabank Arena in Toronto, home of the Toronto Maple Leafs, and there was a young girl next to our bench who had a sign that said, KENDALL NEXT YEAR YOU WILL BEAT ALL THE BOYS! #ALLSTARSKILLS2020 #GIRLPOWER. The moment was so big, and while both of these young girls may have been cheering for Canada, the rivalry didn't matter in this respect. It was a win for our sport, and one that will be a part of hockey history forever. My skates from the Fastest Skater Competition will be a part of hockey history as well—at their new home, the Hockey Hall of Fame. I didn't try to call my parents for permission this time.

People ask me all the time if I was nervous when I skated in the Fastest Skater Competition, and the answer is yes. But I truly believe nerves are a good thing because they mean you care deeply. Nerves can be a bad thing only if you don't know how to con- trol them and you let them take over when you're under pressure. Instead, I use them to fuel my drive to be the best I can be. I was either going to crush that moment or that moment was going to crush me and, even bigger than me, the sport. Because I jumped on that opportunity, I was able to accomplish something beyond it.

"Pressure is a privilege."

—*BILLIE JEAN KING*

NOT DONE YET

Every day is a day to create change,
be better, and make history.

*I*n April 2019, I competed in my seventh World Championships. Before the tournament began, a group of American and Canadian players met to discuss the future of the women's professional game. We were so tired of accepting the crumbs: sleeping on air mattresses at friends' houses or sleeping three to a room at hotels, getting our own pre-game meals, practicing only twice a week if it worked alongside our work schedule, making as little as $2,000 a year, and playing for a team in a location where we found a full-time job that would allow us to play hockey on the side. In this moment, it didn't matter we were rivals. This conversation was so much bigger than that. Bigger than us. Bigger than the game.

We knew our collective voice would be stronger to advocate for the change this game so desperately needed. We did exactly that once the tournament ended. While there were a lot of distractions going on around women's professional hockey, everyone was able to stay focused on the task at hand. As proof of that, we won our fifth consecutive World Championship, beating Team Finland in a shootout 2–1. There were a few special things about this World Championship. Because of our 2017 boycott, we received our first guest fund, and most players had someone there to support them. It was wonderful to see. Secondly, it was the first time I was the captain of Team USA in a World Championship. I had been the captain at the Rivalry Series, and that was special, but being a captain at the World Championship, something that was voted on by my teammates, was truly a special honor and responsibility.

There is a lot of work that goes on behind the scenes as a leader. You have to be willing to put the team before yourself but not let your preparation and performance slide. Being awarded the Directorate Award as the best forward of the tournament, and months later being named the Bob Allen Women's Player of the Year by USA Hockey, not only proved to myself that I could handle the many different hats I was wearing, it was a moment where I could be proud of myself for the work I had put in. It is not easy waking up every day, finding your own ice, finding your weight room time, and constantly pushing yourself to be better— alone. Women's hockey is done being alone.

On May 2, 2019, history was made once again when we formed the Professional Women's Hockey Players Association (PWHPA). Two hundred of the best players in the world came together to fight for a sustainable and viable women's professional league. We had no money, no structure. Once again, in order to make history, you have to know history. When you think of *the* champion for gender equality, it's Billie Jean King. When you watch tennis, and you see men and women receiving equal prize money—that's because of Billie Jean King. I grew up knowing I could get a full scholarship and play college hockey because Title IX prohibits sex-based discrimination in any school or other education program that receives federal money—that's because of Billie Jean King. It didn't happen because she asked politely. She had to be willing to risk everything. She had to fight. She had to sacrifice. She was willing to do it for future generations—like mine. It's now our turn.

I was honored to be able to call Billie Jean King and her partner, Ilana Kloss, to ask for advice. One phone call has turned into too many to count at this point. They have been willing to provide the PWHPA with an enormous amount of advice, time, work, and support.

We also once again sought help from Ballard Spahr, who came through. They provided more pro bono work and legal counsel to help us set up the governance of the players' association we'd just formed. The Professional Women's Hockey Players Association has been active and thriving ever since, partnering with NHL clubs to host the Dream Gap Tour. The name comes from the desire to close the gap between what a young boy can dream to become versus a young girl in the sport of hockey.

We made multiple stops in Chicago in partnership with the Chicago Blackhawks, which I am very proud of. We even got to play in the United Center and became the first women's hockey game to ever to be played at Madison Square Garden in New York City! We also had stops in San Jose, St. Louis, Philadelphia, Calgary, Toronto, and Arizona—all alongside the cities' NHL clubs. The PWHPA captured a historical one-million-dollar commitment from Secret Deodorant so the players' work and voice continue to pay off. The fight for our worth is not just for us; it is for the four-year-old girl who now plays hockey after seeing me skate at the All-Star Weekend, and all of the other young hockey players who will come after us. We don't want them to be us, we want them to be better than us, but they need to be treated like it first.

Shortly after, I was offered to join the San Jose Sharks' broadcast team as an analyst. San Jose is where so many magical moments in my life have occurred. Michael won the Super Bowl there, I skated in the Skills Competition there, and I got offered my first job in broadcasting there. I learned so much that year and was really lucky to be surrounded by so many incredible mentors. Unfortunately, the season was cut short due to COVID-19, but I was very honored to be an analyst for a city that adopted me as one of their own since January 25, 2019.

In January 2019, Michael and I formed the Schofield Family Foundation. Both of us are incredibly passionate about being connected to the community and giving back in as many ways as possible. We have five focus areas that spoke to us when we formed the foundation: first responders; families in need; military; youth sports; education and research. The NHL actually surprised us on that same momentous All-Star Weekend with $25,000 to donate to the charity of our choice. That gave our foundation its first life and the chance to get started doing some of the things we set out to do.

A couple months later, we were able to give away our first-ever annual scholarship to a Carl Sandburg student athlete who was going on to play sports at the next level. It was special and so meaningful that we could impact the life of a fellow Carl

Sandburg student athlete who would be going on to do amazing things. Shortly thereafter, we made a $50,000 commitment to the Ronald McDonald House in Oak Lawn to provide a room for the families who are in need.

In 2020, I played in my second Rivalry Series. We played two games in Canada, including one in Vancouver, and that was great because we all got to have dinner at Cammi's house. On February 8, little did I know I would be playing in my last game of 2020 and wouldn't put on the USA jersey until August 2021. We played in Anaheim, at Honda Center. My parents came; Jake was able to take a leave from the Army to join. In total, 13,320 people attended, and we broke the record for the most fans in a Women's National Team game on US soil—once again proving our worth.

On March 8, 2020, I was part of the first all-women's NBC Sports broadcast crew at my home rink when the Blackhawks played the St. Louis Blues. NBC Sports put together a "super team" that happened to all be women to run the game, from the camera operators to the producer, director, and then the ones they call "talent" (a term I've never understood, because everyone on the broadcast team is talented!), myself and 1998 Olympic gold medalist A.J. Mleczko as analysts and Kate Scott on play-by-play. I was inside the glass for the game, and it was another first of something and another spectacular moment that opened the eyes and doors for other girls and women to see what they can become. It was extra special for me to call this game at home. Three days later, the whole world shut down due to the COVID-19 pandemic.

Since 2013, I'd continued to love my work in the community with the Blackhawks. Because I had been active with them and had successes on and off the ice, in October 2020 I was hired as the first-ever female player development coach and youth hockey growth specialist. Shortly after, Michael and I became a part of the ownership group of the Chicago Red Stars in the National Women's Soccer League. Being able to be a part of an ownership group for our hometown women's professional soccer team has been one of our proudest accomplishments. We know how important it is to invest in women's sports, and to be able to do so in our hometown, with the Red Stars, allows us to help create change we need to see in women's professional sports overall.

While the sport of hockey has come a long way since I was a little girl, in spite of everything I've accomplished—and even though I have had so many more opportunities in this sport than those who came before me—I know I have to prove myself all the time to ensure there are even more opportunities for those who come after me. Even if others continue to say that I'm not enough, I will continue to prove I am. This constant fight has prepared me for anything. I'm always ready to be the first to do things. It has definitely made me want to make sure I'm not the last.

For me, it started with a pair of skates and a dream. Because of the love and passion I had for a sport I found at three years old, which only grew as I got older, I was able to become an Olympian, a world champion, a coach, a broadcaster, an owner, a philanthropist, and become the first to do so many other things on and off the ice.

None of it would have happened without my love for the sport and the resiliency, work ethic, attitude, and burning desire and drive to be the best I can be along the way. It wouldn't have happened without the support of so many people, including my coaches, teammates, friends, and ultimately my family. I will be forever grateful for the people I have encountered throughout my journey. The truth is, no one expected me to be so successful in a sport that was deemed only appropriate for boys. We can be many things, and we should be as many things as we want to be. Remember, you and only you determine who you are and what you can dream to become. If you know what you want and you go for it without hesitation no matter what the world throws your way, you can end up on top.

The wins and losses are one thing, but my experiences, my memories, my education, traveling the world, representing my country, and meeting my closest friends are the greatest gifts hockey has given me.

While I have many goals and dreams I still hope to accomplish, there is one on the forefront of my mind and efforts every day, and that is working toward the vision of a women's professional hockey league that is sustainable, viable, and allows women in professional hockey to make a living doing it so that young boys and young girls can grow up with the same dream. I want anyone reading this to know: fight for the things that are important to you too. Listen to your heart and you too can break down barriers along the way. No dream is too big. Set your own pace to accomplish them. I hope my journey has prepared you in some small way. You might want to do some of the things I've done, but I challenge you to do more, to find something you believe in and take it all the way.

While success isn't guaranteed to anyone, there are things you can do every day to get closer to where you want to be and what you want to achieve. And when you do reach the goal you've been working toward, use whatever platform you've gained to help someone else striving for their goals. I wouldn't be where I am today without everyone who saw my passion and drive and then helped me grow into the person I am today. I hope you find those same people in your life—and become that person to someone else as well.

Because together, anything is possible.

HOCKEY HISTORY TIMELINE

1956—Abby Hoffman challenges the gender barrier in hockey by pretending to be a boy in order to play on a boys' team

1965—Brown University establishes the first women's college hockey team

June 23, 1972—Title IX is enacted, which is an educational amendment prohibiting federally funded educational institutions from discriminating against students or employees based on sex

1976—First Ivy League tournament

1984—First ECAC tournament

1987—An unofficial Women's World Championship is played in Toronto, Canada

March 19-25, 1990—The first International Ice Hockey Federation–sanctioned tournament in women's ice hockey— the Women's World Championships—takes place in Ottawa, Ontario, Canada

May 25, 1992—Kendall is born

September 23, 1992—Manon Rhéaume becomes the first woman to play in any of the major North American sports leagues when she plays goalie for the first-year Tampa Bay Lightning in a preseason game against the St. Louis Blues

1994—Minnesota becomes the first state in the US to sanction women's ice hockey as a high school varsity sport

October 20-27, 1996—The Three Nations Cup tournament is formed between Team USA, Team Canada, and Team Finland, and takes place in various locations in Ontario and Canton, New York

1998—The Patty Kazmaier Memorial Award is created to annually honor the top women players in NCAA DI Women's College Hockey. The award is named to honor standout Princeton student athlete Patty Kazmaier (1981–1986), who lost her battle with a rare blood disease on February 15, 1990. Her father, Dick Kazmaier, won the Heisman Trophy in 1951.

February 7-17, 1998—The XVIII Winter Olympic Games in Nagano, Japan, host the first-ever Women's Hockey Tournament at the Olympic Games. On February 17, 1998, the United States captures a gold medal in a 3–1 win over Team Canada.

November 7-11, 2000—The Three Nations Cup Tournament becomes the Four Nations Cup Tournament when Sweden joins the United States, Canada, and Finland, with games played in Provo, Utah

2001—The NCAA officially sanctions women's hockey and holds the first women's hockey tournament

2002—Women's Hockey East—part of a hockey-only DI NCAA conference—begins

January 5, 2002—Team USA plays Team Canada at the United Center. This is the first time Kendall remembers seeing women play hockey live.

2003—The Women's World Championship in Beijing is cancelled due to concern over Severe Acute Respiratory Syndrome (SARS) in Asia

February 2004—Kendall and her Team Powerade squad make history as the first all-girls team to participate in the Quebec International Pee-Wee Hockey Tournament

2007—The International Ice Hockey Federation announces they are starting the U18 Women's World Championships

January 7-12, 2008—Kendall plays in the first-ever U18 Women's World Championship in Calgary, Alberta, Canada

January 5-10, 2009—Kendall plays in the second U18 Women's World Championship in Fussen, Germany

March 27-April 3, 2010—Kendall competes in the third U18 Women's World Championship in Woodridge, Illinois. This is the first time the U18 Women's World Championships is held on US soil.

November 8, 2010—Cammi Granato and Angela James become the first women inducted into the Hockey Hall of Fame

April 2-9, 2013—Kendall competes in the IIHF Women's World Championship in Ottawa, Canada, where Team USA wins gold over Team Canada

February 7-22, 2014—Kendall competes in her first Olympics, held in Sochi, Russia, where Team USA wins silver in the final game against Team Canada

March 28-April 4, 2015—Kendall competes in the IIHF Women's World Championship in Malmō, Sweden, where Team USA wins gold against Team Russia

March 28-April 4, 2016—Kendall competes in the IIHF

Women's World Championship in Kamloops, Canada, where Team USA wins gold over Team Canada

January 14, 2017—The University of Wisconsin breaks a record for the most attended NCAA DI women's hockey game with 15,359 people watching in their stadium

March 15, 2017—Team USA announces they will boycott the World Championships on home soil in the midst of their battle with USA Hockey for equitable treatment. At that time, Team USA was ranked number one in the world.

March 29, 2017—Three days before the start of the World Championships, USA Hockey agrees to give male and female Team USA players the same benefits, as well as agrees to pay the women's team on par with the men's team

March 31–April 7, 2017—Kendall competes in the IIHF Women's World Championship in Plymouth Township, Michigan, where Team USA again wins gold over Team Canada

February 9–24, 2018—Kendall competes in her second Olympics, where Team USA wins their first gold in twenty years after a historic overtime shootout against Team Canada

January 25, 2019—Kendall becomes the first woman to compete in the NHL All-Star Skills competition

February 2019—The Rivalry Series, a three-game series between Team USA and Team Canada, is formed

April 4–14, 2019—Kendall competes in the IIHF Women's World Championship in Espoo, Finland, where Team USA captures its fifth consecutive Worlds gold in a shootout win against Team Finland; in her first year as team captain, Kendall is awarded Best Forward of the tournament

May 2, 2019—The Professional Women's Hockey Players Association is formed to promote, advance, and support a single, viable professional women's ice hockey league in North America that showcases the greatest product of women's professional ice hockey in the world

July 2019—Kendall becomes the first woman to play in the Chicago Pro Hockey League (CPHL), a summer league in Chicago

September 5, 2019—Kendall joins the San Jose Sharks broadcast team as the team's first female color analyst

September 13, 2019—The Swedish Ice Hockey Federation—hosts of the 2019 Four Nations Cup—cancels the Four Nations Tournament because players are boycotting due to unfair pay and work conditions. The tournament has yet to be played again.

February 8, 2020—A record crowd of 13,320 shows up at the Honda Center in Anaheim, California, to watch the US Women's National Team play Team Canada

March 7, 2020—The International Ice Hockey Federation cancels the 2020 Women's World Championships due to the COVID-19 pandemic

March 8, 2020—The first all-female crew works a game on NBC Sports between the St. Louis Blues and the Chicago Blackhawks. Kendall is inside the glass as an analyst for the game.

November 23, 2020—Kendall becomes the first female player development coach in Chicago Blackhawks history, becoming a member of the team she hoped to play for as a child

February 28, 2021—Kendall plays in the first-ever women's professional hockey game—held at the iconic Madison Square Garden in New York, New York—as a member of the Professional Women's Hockey Players Association. Her Team Adidas faced Team Women's Sports Foundation.

April 24, 2021—Due to the ongoing COVID-19 pandemic, the International Ice Hockey Federation announces it is canceling the 2021 Women's World Championships that were scheduled to be played May 6–16, 2021

May 14, 2021—Kendall is behind the bench as an assistant coach for a game with the Rockford Icehogs, the American Hockey League Affiliate for the Chicago Blackhawks—the first woman to serve in that position for the team

August 20-31, 2021—Kendall competes in the rescheduled 2021 IIHF Women's World Championship played in Calgary, Alberta, Canada; Team USA wins silver in the final against Team Canada

October 2021–February 2022—Kendall trains alongside Team USA for the 2022 Winter Olympics in Beijing, China

To date—No women's professional hockey league exists that gives women the opportunity to make a living playing the game

Beyond—Barriers will continue to be broken

ACKNOWLEDGMENTS

*I*t all started with a pair of figure skates that soon turned into hockey skates. My love for being in those skates took me on an amazing journey. This was possible because of the world's greatest family, friends, mentors, and supporters. Each one has played a pivotal role in providing me with the love, support, guidance, and encouragement I needed to pursue my dreams. Here are just a few that I'd like to thank:

Mom and Dad: Thank you for your unconditional love and support for any dream I thought was possible. You showed the true definition of working hard and never giving up. Your dedication and sacrifices have allowed me to do what I love. I wouldn't be who I am today without you, and I hope someday I become a wonderful parent as well. I love you more than anything.

Kevin, Jake, and Bailey: Thank you for your love, support, unique humor, and friendship. Kevin—thank you for always allowing your little sister to look up to you and follow you around, and never taking it easy on me no matter what competition we were having. Jake and Bailey—thank you for being the best little brother and sister anyone could ask for. I am so proud of everything you have accomplished.

I love you all!

Michael: Thank you for always being my biggest fan literally and figuratively, in sports and in life. I love you.

Mackenzie Nagle: From the very beginning, thank you for always supporting my dreams and ambitions, especially when many others didn't.

Amanda Boskovich (Bosko): You are always there for me no matter what, when, how, why, or where. Thank you for being such a loyal friend.

Billie Jean King and Ilana Kloss: You have spent your lives making this world a better place for everyone and have impacted my life in so many ways. I am thankful to have seen your self-lessness, your sacrifice, your grit, your willingness to never give up, and your incredible endurance to help others fight for what is right. You are *always* there to provide me with advice, support, and tough love when I need it most. I am forever grateful for your friendship and inspiration—it truly is one of the greatest honors and privileges of my life.

Cammi Granato: Thank you for being the best: pioneer, game changer, leader, role model, and inspiration. You ignited a dream for the next generation, including me, and changed my life because of it. Thank you for showing me what it means to leave the game better than you found it. I am so grateful for your friendship and mentorship to this day.

Annie Camins: Thank you for bringing me onto the team I always dreamed to join. Even though I didn't play for the Blackhawks, you saw the value in bringing this hometown kid in as a community ambassador and attend events alongside the Blackhawk stars, showing both young boys and girls who they could become. Because of your advocacy for girls and women in hockey, your leadership, and your experience, it has been an honor to work alongside you, creating more accessible and affordable opportunities for youth hockey players in Illinois, including the Golden Coynes program. Without your belief in me, I would not be where I am today. I am so thankful for your, Mike's, and Amelia's friendship.

Manon Rhéaume: Thank you for your fight to create more opportunities for the next generation of girls in hockey. I am so thankful for all the advice and support you've provided me throughout my career. Dylan and Dakota have the best role model in their mom.

Patrick Burke: We need more allies like you in this world. Leaders who challenge the status quo, and stand up and speak out for what they believe in. You believed in me when no one else did, and the impact from that moment is still being felt in the sport of hockey and the role of girls and women within it. I am so thankful for your and Caiti's friendship.

To all my teammates: Thank you for challenging me to be the best version of myself and holding me accountable to be the best teammate I can be. To all my teammates who continue to stand up and fight for the future of this game—our collective voice is powerful.

I want to give a special thanks to all the boys' teams I have practiced with since I graduated from college, including the Chicago Mission, Colorado Thunderbirds, and Anaheim Jr. Ducks. Without your support, I would not have been able to practice with a team in between National Team commitments. Thank you for helping me prepare for whatever was next.

The Team Behind the Team: My strength coaches, doctors,

athletic trainers, physical therapists, massage therapist, nutritionists, mental skills coaches, equipment managers, and video coordinators—thank you for your relentless commitment to my career. You have allowed me to give my very best every single day—even at times when I am not at my best, you are *always* at your best.

To all my coaches: Thank you for seeing the love and passion I had in this sport, nurturing it, and allowing it to grow. Thank you for caring about me as a person first and a hockey player second. The greatest compliment I can give to you is that I followed in your footsteps and became a coach myself.

Ballard Spahr—John Langel, Dee Spagnuolo, and all the partners and associates at Ballard Spahr who have dedicated their time, knowledge, and expertise to women's hockey: Thank you for believing in our fight, making our voices heard, and advocating for the change the women's game so desperately needs. We would not be where we are today without your unparalleled commitment. You have changed our lives, and together we will leave the game better than we found it.

My Blackhawks family: Thank you for allowing me to be a part of this special family in so many different ways—from a Jr. Blackhawk fan, to an intern, to an ambassador, to a player development coach and youth hockey growth specialist. It is an honor and privilege. To the Emmy Award–winning team of the documentary *As Fast As Her*, your amazing work inspired the title and cover for this book, and for that I thank you.

My broadcasting family: To *everyone* I have worked with from NBC Sports, NBC Sports California, and NHL Network in my broadcasting career—thank you for believing in me, and for being such wonderful friends, supporters, and teammates. To my broadcasting agent, Lou Oppenheim, thank you for your love and support and always knowing how to make me smile.

Barbara Perry, my agent at Billie Jean King Enterprises: Thank you for helping me manage my crazy life and always having my best interest at heart.

Tip Nunn: Thank you for being willing to step up to the plate and knock it out of the park as the publicist for the book.

Frank Weimann, my literary agent: Thank you for your help to make this book a reality.

Estelle Laure: Thank you for listening to my journey and helping craft it into a story that will be an inspiration for both kids and adults.

My book team: Thank you to everyone at Zondervan and HarperCollins who believed in me and my story. Thank you for accommodating my crazy schedule. A special thanks to my publisher, Megan Dobson, and Kate Jacobs and Jacque Alberta for editing the manuscript. And much appreciation goes to Sara Merritt, the senior director of marketing; Jessica Westra, my publicist at Zondervan; as well as to the art director, the photo editor, the typesetter, and the incredible sales force.

Family, friends, fans, and the next generation: Thank you for always believing in me.

For more information about Kendall, or to connect with her online, visit:

Website: www.kendallcoyne.com

 Facebook: @KendallCoyne26

 Instagram: @kendallcoyne26

 Twitter: @kendallcoyne

ABOUT THE AUTHOR

Kendall Coyne Schofield is a professional hockey player and Olympian who won gold and silver medals while representing Team USA. In 2019, she became the first woman to compete in the NHL All-Star Skills Competition, where she finished less than a second behind the winner, Connor McDavid, in the Fastest Skater Competition. Currently, Kendall lives in Orland Park, Illinois, with her husband, NFL player Michael Schofield, and their dog, Blue.